A Table for Three Please
The Rainbow Years

Jeremy Lawley Fell

A Table for Three Please
The Rainbow Years

Vanguard Press

A CIP catalogue record for this title is
available from the British Library.

ISBN 978 1 80016 889 3

*Vanguard Press is an imprint of
Pegasus Elliot Mackenzie Publishers Ltd.*
www.pegasuspublishers.com

First Published in 2023

**Vanguard Press
Sheraton House Castle Park
Cambridge England**

Printed & Bound in Great Britain

Introduction

This book is written as a tribute to my late wife and dedicated to our lives together. She sadly passed away in 2016 after a really wonderful forty-two years together. This is the first part of my book 'A Table for Three Please' which compares my life as a London University student in the 1960s with my daughter Pamela's who studied at Loughborough University and graduated in 2008. I have had a very successful career in both the private and public sectors and I hope that you will find it both informative and amusing. I have met some amazing people, many of whom have become multi-millionaires and are now household names. The fascination of the rainbow will also be explained later. Please note, where appropriate, I have depersonalised some of the names to protect their identity.

Judith & Jeremy 2010

Profile of the Author

Born Jeremy Lawley Fell at Birmingham Children's Hospital he was a typical post-war baby! Small and underweight but he developed quickly with the help of his mum and dad.

He lived with his middle-class parents in a new house on an estate in Erdington and his dad travelled each day to his insurance job in central Birmingham. He was a typical Thursday born boy who had 'far to go' in life. His early days at Yenton Primary School were not good and he remembered at the end of the first term his position in the class was forty-six. There were forty-seven in his group of both girls and boys – every day was a struggle! The headmaster said that he was 'not an academic boy' but following intervention from his dad, he would still put him on the list to take the 11+ examination. This he failed.

Later in his life he met someone who had a similar problem. However, they both in their own ways changed the world. The turning point came when he was just eleven years old when he received a Lott's Chemistry Set for his birthday. This changed his life and he became interested in science.

A year later, his parents sent him to a private school called Wylde Green College, Sutton Coldfield, in the county of Warwickshire. (now West Midlands)

Most of the staff wore black gowns and the boys maroon blazers and ties with the Latin inscription 'Ego, regem sequar, follow the king.(of heaven).

Following his interest in science, he took A-Level GCEs in chemistry, physics and pure maths at Handsworth Technical College in Birmingham. In 1965 he moved to London and studied for a BSc honours Degree in Analytical Chemistry. The course included two years in industry at Albright and Wilson Laboratories based in Oldbury in Worcestershire (now West Midlands). His research project was on NMRS (Nuclear Magnetic Resonance Spectroscopy) as an analytical tool.

Professor Peter Mansfield of Nottingham University was also working on the same technology and he came up with the idea of using similar equipment to scan the human body for muscles and tissues. In 1971 Jeremy met him at Imperial College, London and they discussed ideas including their school days and both of them failing their 11+ exams.

Peter tested equipment and began to perfect nuclear magnetic resonance body scanning, later dropping the word 'nuclear' because of people's perception of this linking it to atomic bombs.

Magnetic Resonance Image Scanning was born!

Today almost every hospital in the world has one which has saved many hundreds of thousands of lives! Vets also use them on animals. Peter died in 2017 aged 83 but was knighted by the Queen and received the Nobel Prize for Medicine in 2003 for his work on MRSI. After university, Jeremy felt that chemistry was not his future and secured a job as a chemical buyer which included international travel, particularly to Eastern Europe. He was very successful and soon progressed to also include engineering and general buying. He even travelled across 'Check Point Charlie' from East to West Berlin. He also became a Member of the Chartered Institute of Purchasing and Supply (MCIPS) in 1976.

In 1979 he joined Dudley Metropolitan Borough Council as Purchasing Manager, the first at any authority in the Midlands, and shortly after, Chairman of the Black Country Purchasing Consortium on behalf of Dudley, Sandwell, Walsall and Wolverhampton councils, responsible for a spend of £100 million – a lot of money back then! They are still going today.

Later he joined Birmingham City Council as City Purchasing Manager with a spend with his team of around 120 staff, approaching £950 million, today's equivalent of probably £5 billion or more! They also furnished and equipped the NEC, ICC, NIA and Birmingham's Symphony Hall.

He also became a member of the Major Energy Users Council in London and Chairman of their Energy Efficiency and the Environment Committee.

He spoke at many conferences on the environment including one with John Craven of BBC's Countryfile in Birmingham. Further details of which he has referred to in this book. He also chaired a meeting in the House of Lords in London on 'The Environment', amazing but scary as he was understandably nervous at the time.

In 1992, following a tough interview he was appointed as Head of Purchasing & Administration for TSB Bank based at their HQ at Victoria House, Victoria Square in Birmingham. They also had offices in Andover, Brighton, Manchester and Glasgow. He was appointed director of TSB print and design services Ltd in the City of London.

Finally, before his retirement from business he formed in 2000 his own company, Lawley Management Consultants, specialists in procurement and cost reduction for major organisations including the NHS, Co-op Bank and The Pertemps Group.

Back to 1956 "the Chemistry set" that changed his life.

Footnote by Simon Fell

At the age of 75 my dad became an author with his first Book *A Table for Three Please – The Rainbow Years*. This was followed by Schrodinger's Change – without the umlaut, then *Graceland Towers*. His latest book *2045 – Tomorrow's World Now* is a fictional tale of life in twenty-three years' time. Could he be right? He is currently working on *It's a Caring World* about care homes of the future.

Chapter 1 – The Rainbow Years

The year 2005 was a good year for us all and we looked to the future with hope. I therefore decided to retire from business early as we were well off, had a lovely house and a loving family. Money was the least of our problems and I had worked very hard during my career and I was very proud of my many achievements. Life could hardly be better and both our children, Simon and Pamela, had partners and had left home. In September 2015, Pamela and her partner Dan got married at the Barbican in London and both Judith and I, plus our guests, could not have been happier. It was a magic occasion!

Shortly after, Judith became ill; she had developed lung cancer. During our forty-two years together she showed no symptoms, although she did get breathless easily. She never smoked, although both our sets of parents did, and also our grandparents. It was the norm in the 1950s after the war years.

My dad had been in the Royal Navy on the Russian convoy to Murmansk and he smoked cigarettes, cigars and a pipe. I cannot remember him without something in his mouth, usually Players 'untipped' Navy Cut. I am a non-smoker now but I do remember trying a few cigarettes in my late teens.

After several sessions of chemotherapy, Judith's cancer was not getting better and it had spread to her bones and brain. She died on 10 August 2016 and had spent time at St Giles Hospice in Whittington. The staff there were so wonderful. Do you know that Judith never complained, even in her last days, despite her pain?

At Judith's funeral, a strange thing happened. It was a warm day with blue skies, no rain and little wind. Afterwards, Dan and Pamela decided to go back and collect some blue flowers from her coffin for drying and pressing.

Then a beautiful rainbow appeared in the sky, pointing back towards our house. Although I did not realise it at the time, this would be the first appearance of many spectrums. (Yes, this is the right spelling!)

We had both always loved the colours and I wondered why this was here. Was she looking over us? I cannot explain.

I have included a photograph of this and other occurrences later in this book. Did you know that the full colours of the spectrum are infrared, red, orange, yellow, green, blue, indigo, violet, and ultraviolet? This I know from my days as a chemist in the late 1960s.

For Judith's funeral, I wrote the Order of Service and also included some of her favourite hymns such as 'Love Divine' and a special reading by the English poet, A. E. Housman (1859-1936) who wrote it after his father had died in 1896. It is a poem steeped in wistfulness and memories of his childhood and the sad loss of his dad.

"Into my heart an air that kills
 From yon far country blows:
What are those blue remembered hills?
What spires, what farms are those?

This is the land of lost content,
I see it shining plain.
The happy highways were I went
And cannot come again."

Simon read this as a tribute to his mum at the small church of St Peter's, in Little Aston, close to our home.

I am, like most people, not a great lover of funerals. But when you have been married and loved someone for such a long time, this is one occasion which will never be forgotten.

I would now like to move on to how I was coping after all these changes to my life, including osteoarthritis. After a short time, I had improved my walking ability and could perform many tasks which would have been impossible earlier.

What I have not mentioned is that on March 5th 2018, it was Pamela's birthday and I did not realise what a day it would be. She was in London but we managed to speak on the phone in the morning and she told me that she was pregnant. Wow, we were all so delighted. I was to have a grandson at last! If only Judith was still around!

It was a cold day and we had snow and frozen ice around; then in the afternoon, in the back garden, I fell backwards and fractured my shoulder badly. I could see my raw bone sticking out! The pain was out of this world and I was taken to hospital. After an x-ray I was operated on the next day. My surgeon installed a titanium plate and attached it to my shoulder bone and then stitched up the fifteen-centimetre wound.

After three months of treatment by a physiotherapist at Little Aston Hospital, I could at last raise my right arm again and all the black and blue bruises had gone. I still had some pains. I thought, could things really get any worse?

For years I had suffered pains in my legs, spine and hands, and despite taking opiate painkillers, even morphine, they continued. I really missed jogging after work each night as it kept me both fit and healthy. After working in an office all day, to get outside was marvellous.

Most of my life I had always enjoyed alcohol, particularly French red wine and Scottish whisky.

It is now over two years since my last drink!

On 25th September 2019, 'horror of horrors', I had two strokes and a heart attack. I was on the floor in the kitchen at home, coughing blood, so my son Simon phoned for an ambulance and I was taken to Good Hope Hospital. This was the last I can remember. I heard later that I was transferred to intensive care for a month, of which I spent several weeks on an oxygen ventilator in an induced coma. The cardiologist told Simon that his dad was very ill and they said that they were doing their best but the prognosis was not good.

After four weeks in intensive care I then went onto the ward and stayed a further seven weeks. I could not walk, was bed bound and had to also wear a catheter. This was really uncomfortable and I needed twenty-four-hour care.

The ambulance guys were so good, as were the team in intensive care. They had saved my life and at one stage my heart had stopped for fifteen, minutes! Flatlining, I think they call it.

In late December 2019, I was therefore transferred to the relatively new Gracewell Care Home, in Sutton Coldfield. I have my own room and en-suite bathroom, plus twenty-four-hour care. Just shortly after I moved in, I had a visit from Jack, my new grandson, who was born at King's College Hospital in London. I only wished Judith had been there as she would have been so proud and happy, as we all are.

Pam and Dan are such good parents! I am impressed. Jack calls her 'Mum'. Little Jack is growing up fast and can talk and make animal noises, particularly cats.

What does their cat, Paul, think? That he is no longer the top dog, sorry, cat? He also does not like Jack pulling his tail. Who would?

My thoughts turned to how lucky I had been. In February, the new COVID-19 virus pandemic started to spread throughout the world.

In 1981, the American thriller author Dean Koontz published his book 'The Eyes Of Darkness', notable now for 'predicting' the COVID-19 global pandemic. In his own words, "In around 2020, a severe pneumonia-like illness will spread throughout the globe, attacking the lungs and bronchial tubes and resisting all known treatments... They call the stuff 'Wuhan 400' because it was developed at their RDNA laboratories outside of the Chinese City of Wuhan".

Is this just a coincidence or an amazing prediction? Either way it is astonishingly accurate! Although whether the virus was man-made remains to be fully proven.

Whatever your view on this and many other conspiracy theories, I think everyone will agree that

2020 was a crazy year with terrible consequences for nearly all of humankind.

The virus has affected nearly every area of life and its effects have touched all people on our planet in some way. In addition to the tragic loss of life, it has impacted us all economically, politically and mentally.

In the UK we had a 'lockdown'. In the beginning, this meant that pretty much everything was closed apart from food shops and also healthcare. It meant that people couldn't go to work, see their friends, go on holiday, eat out or visit older relatives. It meant panic buying of items like toilet rolls, video calls, clapping for carers, one daily walk, social distancing, chats on drives and furlough leave. Furlough leave! I didn't even know that word until 2020!

For many people it meant loneliness, especially the older generation and those with health conditions. Even as lockdown eased for many, some groups have had to continue to 'shield' from society – sometimes for months. This must have been extremely hard to bear.

The virus has changed the culture of society – perhaps permanently. We've almost become used to the 'new normal' of wearing face masks everywhere and queuing for everything with people being two metres apart.

In some ways, perhaps the virus has brought us closer together and made us more caring. People now know their neighbours better and everyone helps each other out a bit more.

We have developed a stronger appreciation for our nurses, carers and cleaners – professions that we used to take for granted and not value as much.

Perhaps the distancing rule has also made us appreciate the value of relationships more than at any time since the Second World War. Hopefully there will be a vaccine soon or the virus will peter out. I also hope that this crisis has brought people together to realise we must value each other and the planet we live on.

The word corona refers to the yellow glow on the outside of our sun, often observed when an eclipse occurs. Please do not look without eye protection. This is also the same as the yellow colours in rainbows and part of the spectrum of white light.

Being unable to move about freely and being stuck in bed all day is not easy and loneliness starts to kick in. Some people could not understand why the government restricted people's movements. I had now been in lockdown for over twelve months! Or as I call it, 'lockup'!

I should shortly like to move on to the second part of my autobiography, which focuses on my main theme, which looks at life as a student back in the 1960s when I first went to university in London to study chemistry and my daughter, Pamela, who went to Loughborough University in 2005 to study graphic design.

Recently, after the start of the COVID-19 virus, in March 2020, concern has been raised about the handling of 'A' level results which I can understand. But when I went to uni, only less than five per cent of young people had that opportunity and 'A' grades were extremely rare. Now they are so common that everyone thinks they deserve special treatment.

Why, may I ask?

I strongly believe that all a degree shows is that you are capable of learning… that alone. Your degree will get you an interview, then if you secure the job it is up to you and the most important things in life are to have confidence and enthusiasm. Never ever accept failure and you will go far. It matters little where you have come from but what you have achieved in life's road.

As the Dutch say, "Het leven is een strijd maar het einddoel is je motivator": "Life can be a struggle but it is the end goal that drives you." I feel that to have also given so much pleasure in helping others and seeing them progress, particularly in my own family, has been very rewarding.

Now let us move back to the year 2005 and the reason for this book, 'A Table for Three Please – The Rainbow Years'.

Chapter 2 – Year 1, Term 1

The day had finally arrived; our daughter Pamela was leaving home to go to university to study for three years and hopefully secure a BA in graphic communications. We left the house, the car all loaded up with clothes, shoes and handbags plus a few essential items such as cooking utensils, plates, cutlery and food etc. The most important item of all, which was double checked as being packed, was her electric hair straighteners.

As we drove up the road, our thoughts turned to how we were going to cope with an empty nest. Indeed, how was she going to cope without us?

The journey was only just forty-seven minutes to Loughborough University Campus, but seemed an age and very little was said during this time. The Beatles' hit of the 1960s 'She's Leaving Home' became very poignant in our minds.

We were of course the first parents to arrive at her new halls of residence, as predicted by Pamela, knowing her father's lifestyle of punctuality.

We were first met by a number of highly enthusiastic second year undergraduates who had organised Fresher's Week. This impressed us but it didn't seem to have any impact on Pamela other than a half-smile.

After registering, while my wife and I had a coffee and biscuits, the time had come to move the vast amount of baggage into her room, which happened to be up two flights of stairs.

Having located the right room and cupboards in the communal kitchen at John Phillips Hall, we proceeded to unpack and Dad was asked to retune her television to pick up stations in the Leicestershire area. I thought at the time how lucky she was to have such luxuries and even her own laptop PC with internet connection (emails are so much easier than writing letters!).

I thought back to my own position back in 1965 when my dad took me down to London, where I began my studies for a BSc degree in chemistry. How different it was!

I was in lodgings with a Mr Sidney and Mrs Ivy Dow in Eltham, South East London. They were in their late fifties and they did not even have a phone as Sid said they couldn't afford it. Really?

To phone home, I had to take a ten-minute walk to the phone box, if it was working, and insert coins into the black box and wait for the line to be connected. On hearing a friendly voice at the other end, usually my mum, I then pressed button 'A' to speak.

If I was lucky I could press button 'B' to get any money left back after the call – old money that was:

shillings and pence. My rent for the week was just six pounds per week, including food and my washing.

The Dows (who no doubt have long since passed away) would be amazed by today's technology with cameras, mobile phones, PCs, iPods, the internet and of course hair straighteners!

In those days we did have black and white TV at my lodgings, which had just two channels: BBC and ITV. It was left on this latter channel all the time, whatever was on! I was fortunate enough to have my own transistor radio and could listen to pirate radio stations like Radio Caroline, Radio London and Radio 390.

My trips back and forward to London were also very different. My father would drop me, usually early evening, at Snow Hill station in Birmingham where I would board the 'steam' train to Paddington. Then on by tube to Charing Cross and forward by main line to Eltham – a journey time of often over four hours in all types of weather.

I remember how cold it was, particularly with thick fog or rather 'smog' hanging over London. The Dows did have central heating but it was rarely on as Sid said, "We can't afford it." Yes, how lucky are today's students!

The car park outside Pamela's hall, block H, which I had christened 'Cell Block H', was now starting to fill up and 'freshers' and their parents were starting to cart quantities of luggage up to their rooms.

I then realised that we were perhaps not alone in bringing so much stuff and to my surprise, flat screen televisions, DVD players, computers/printers and huge quantities of luxury food items were being transported to their new locations. Some students even brought their own forms of transport. How different the world is today!

With all this activity, I felt that it was time for a spot of lunch so off we went to the local inn for a bit of liquid sustenance and food. Pamela, who had not said much for a while, was happy with this and really did not mind where we went as she had passed caring about the future. There was no future!

As we parked the car, I felt this was the end of an era for all of us and life would never be quite the same again. We had seen our only daughter grow up, take her first steps, first days at school and then move on to secondary school and the sixth form.

I remember how she had cried for two days when we arranged for her to go to an independent school rather than the local comprehensive where most of her friends were moving to from the primary school.

She had no friends on day one and it looked as though history was being repeated. What a terrible dad I was! However, she quickly settled into her new school and has since made many good friends, no doubt those who will remain in contact for many years to come.

But going to university was different and she would not be coming back each evening to her mum, dad and older brother who several years ago also went to university – but at the time it seemed less traumatic. Boys cannot show their feelings!

It took me back again to that poem which I had learnt at school many years ago by Mr Housman.

Into my heart an air that kills
From yon far country blows:
What are those blue remembered hills?
What spires, what farms are those?

That is the land of lost content,
I see it shining plain.
The happy highways where I went
And cannot come again.

I recently read this same poem at Gracewell Care Home on Remembrance Day, 11th November.

Pamela had trod many 'happy highways' and all that was about to change.

As we entered the restaurant, we asked the waitress for 'a table for three please', as we had done for many years when our daughter joined us for meals out.

However something was different in this inn and as I gazed round I was struck by the numbers of tables of three. As more parents with their daughters and sons arrived, the same question was asked: a table for three please?

Not all the tables had fathers and mothers and in some cases it was a grandparent attending – perhaps the other parent had to work on this 'freshers' day? The saying 'two's company and three's a crowd' did not obviously apply here! We looked at the menu in silence and made our choices but none of us felt really hungry, least of all Pamela.

Making small talk, I said that she would be able to come here with friends when she had settled into her new hall. Her only comment was that she doubted that she would be able to afford such a luxury and anyway she would probably be back home next week anyway.

Following our meal, we left and went back to her hall and continued to finish her unpacking but the time was rapidly approaching when we had to say our goodbyes and drive home. How would we manage without Pamela?

By this time her hall was starting to fill up and by the faces of those parents and new undergraduates I could tell that these were very anxious times! I had read that the dropout rate for new students was around six per cent – was my daughter likely to be one of those?

My parting comments were that she had worked so hard to gain a place at Loughborough, it was only right that she stayed at least a few weeks. Secretly I had my doubts but said nothing.

I think that life is full of changes and challenges but we do need to understand that we gain so much from these experiences. We become more 'balanced' as the

Japanese say. Wouldn't life seem dull and long if all went right and nothing wrong?

We were rapidly approaching the time for our departure and return home without our daughter, after over twenty years together.

We said our goodbyes to Pamela, gave her a hug and left wishing her 'all the best' in her new student life and saying we would call her later. We drove back home in silence to our empty house. For years I had complained about her loud music, spending hours in the bathroom, being on the phone for ages, leaving her room in a mess, plus the usual teenage moods which is all part of growing up, but on this occasion we would have all of these problems back. The house was so quiet without her. Even the sounds of the Kaiser Chiefs or Coldplay would have been good! The next twenty-four hours were the most difficult and my thoughts turned to the 'what if' scenario should she decide to come home. Was this an option? What would she tell her friends? What we would we tell our friends? How cruel life can be.

Slowly things began to change, with the panic calls saying 'how can I cope' to 'I am so lonely that I don't know what to do next' – and that was just from me! However, Pamela's life was changing and she was beginning to come to terms with being a student and began to realise that she was not alone. She had made new friends who felt just as insecure as her with the changes.

Also at her hall of residence she had come to terms with the fact that if she left an article of clothing on the floor of her room it was still there when she got back.

Finance for university students has changed a lot since my days back in the sixties. Back then, my parents had to apply to the local authority for a grant, which was means tested. This was then paid to me each term and supplemented by my dad.

I did have a bank account but it was a cash society in those days as credit and debit cards had yet to be invented.

I remember opening my account at the Woolwich branch of National Westminster Bank and how kind the bank manager was to me. He also had a son at university and knew how I felt, particularly in the early days. Whenever he saw me, he stopped what he was doing and came across to speak with me and ask if all was going well. This continued throughout my three years' stay in London. I doubt if any students today even know the name of their local bank manager, let alone have met him or her.

Most bank managers are now female, which was rare in the 1960s.

Also in the sixties, excluding mortgages, few people and particularly students had loans other than bank overdrafts. However, I did leave university with no debts which at the time I did not fully appreciate. What debts would Pamela have?

One of the most important things I have learnt in life was from my university tutor in London, who said, "However bright and intelligent you are, the ability to fill in forms is paramount." This applies from the moment you're born until you die. This again was brought home when I applied for a student loan for Pamela. As most parents like me will know, filling in a student loan form is by no means an easy job. Also the first form sent to the Student Loans Company went missing but after several attempts, they managed to eventually confirm details of the payments. Of course all this money would have to be paid back one day when she was earning over fifteen thousand per year. When, I wondered?

As the days and weeks passed, her confidence and state of mind improved and having raised the issue with other parents, we understood that it is normal for daughters and sons to be homesick in the first few weeks.

Having fellow students in similar positions, I believe, helps deal with the problem, but in anything new in life there's always a fear of the unknown and a fear of failure. But a problem shared is problem halved! As Cardinal Newman once said, "A man would do nothing, if he waited until he could do it so well that no one would find fault with what he had done." How true!

It is interesting to note that students' expectations are much higher now than when I was in London. Take entertainment, for example. Yes, we had a Students'

Union and the usual clubs and societies etc. Every Saturday night, there was a disco and several times a term we had major bands playing, which back then were called groups, like the Stones, Beatles, Manfred Mann, the Searchers and many more. The university band circuit has always been there but there are so many more now that the students are spoilt for choice.

I met many famous stars, including the Beatles, when I helped them with their sound system during their visit to Maney Church Hall here in Sutton Coldfield on Friday 1st February 1963. (Did you know that singer Buddy Holly, aged 22, died in an air crash in Clear Lake, USA on 3rd February back in 1959?) Later that night in Sutton Coldfield, Paul McCartney actually introduced himself to me. The next night they played their first UK gig outside Liverpool, in Tamworth!

Later, when I told my wife Judith about this event, she was absolutely amazed as she loved the Beatles so much. The following year they had a mega hit with their disc 'She Loves You' which they also performed at a concert in New York.

Back to students. I understand the Union bar has also expanded. Back in the 1960s, students drank mainly beer and perhaps cider but now it also includes wines and I understand vodka shots.

Freshers like Pamela were even given a shot glass as part of their introduction pack! I often wonder if she ever used it as she was not keen on spirits like whisky, gin or vodka, unlike her dad!

I am not suggesting that we did not drink as university undergraduates forty years ago but it appears that this is a prerequisite for today's students. And of course there are drugs and again these were around in the sixties – being chemistry students we even tried to make our own hallucinogenic substance, LSD, also known today as 'acid'. The chemical name is lysergic acid diethylamide, which was not difficult to produce but we dared not actually try it. Others might have! For those with a scientific background, we analysed the substance with an infrared spectrometer and it was of high quality.

Some of today's students I expect find it a little difficult to handle alcohol and drugs, but who am I to judge?

Governments worldwide need to address this important issue of drug abuse and also the increase in gun-related crimes. The problem is a major concern all over the world and is now equivalent to the topic of nuclear bomb attacks back in the 1960s.

Loughborough, being a top university for sport, has close connections with the Athletic Union and out of this came Wednesday night's club at the Union, 'Hey Ewe' with a number of events, such as the infamous 'totty spotting' which identifies all female students on the campus! The Students' Union building is also more like a shopping mall with bars, shops and restaurants. There are also many services available on campus such as doctors, dentists, banks, supermarkets, debt advisors and many more.

The university has a radio station: LCR (Loughborough Campus Radio) and TV channel: LSUTV (Loughborough Students Union Television).

We did not have the latter but back in London in 1966, I was a DJ for a time at a local radio station: 'Radio Coffee Bar'. I remember my ditty was saying, "Music while you munch all through lunch."

This was at the same time as pirate radio stations like Radio London, 390 and Radio Caroline broadcasted 'illegally'. Caroline was broadcast from a Panamanian registered vessel moored off the Essex coast with a DJ, a Mr Simon Dee. It was an Irish company licensed by a Liechtenstein business to sell commercial airtime.

The prime minister at the time, Alec Douglas Home, sent a gunboat out to Caroline and when Harold Wilson set up government, he instigated the Marine Broadcasting Offences Act and the so-called pirates were outlawed. Shortly after its closure, 'wonderful Radio 1' started with Tony Blackburn (an ex-pirate DJ). Yes, those were exciting times!

Student diets have also changed and become more sophisticated since the 1960s, when such delicacies as beans on toast, sausage and mash with gravy, beef burgers, meat pies and fried chips were the norm.

Chicken and pasta dishes, meat and vegetables were regarded as luxury items, although they were consumed occasionally, on high days and holidays.

Oven chips had not been invented and baguettes were something that the French ate and if on sale were not cheap. Although available, tomatoes, cucumbers and salad products were even more expensive! What will happen after Brexit I wonder?

In the winter months, I remember my landlady Mrs Dow, who used to shop at the 'new' Sainsbury's in Eltham, said you could just not get salads. You could but they were not cheap. The one dish that has always been popular then and still now, is fish and chips. Being close to East London, we did have jellied eels but it was not a popular choice then for us from north of Watford!

I have heard that some of today's students' mothers actually shop for their sons and daughters and fill up their store cupboards and fridges – what luxury. The buzz word is 'helicopter mothers' – a new breed of obsessed parent who refuses to let her children take responsibility for their lives.

How can children learn to become balanced adults? The university years can give young people a unique strength to handle themselves and their offspring in the future! One has to let go, as I keep telling Pamela.

Shopping for food can also be a new experience for students and cooking can also become a daunting prospect. How long should you defrost a chicken breast, how long does bread keep for and why is it that bananas and crisps disappear so quickly?

Thank heavens for a mobile phone to ask mum when cooking questions arise. "Jamie Oliver is soo good – he makes it look simple but what am I doing wrong?"

I remember in my student days, when three of us moved into a house together for my final year, shopping at four forty-five p.m. on a Saturday afternoon when Sainsbury's in those days closed at five p.m. and everything was sold off cheaply – Sunday lunch with a huge pork or beef joint was a day to remember although we often got the cooking time wrong – but you soon learned from your mistakes.

Student clothing styles have changed a lot and I wonder how many guys would now attend lectures wearing a sports jacket, shirt and tie. Jeans were for wearing on special occasions like the Saturday night disco. I would not like to admit to many people that I often wore the same shirts and even underpants for several days or more.

Showers were also rare and it was the norm to have just one bath a week in most London homes, unlike now when I have a shower in the morning and a bath at night! Still, in those days we did not appear to smell or perhaps we just didn't notice it!

My prize possession in the 1960s was a dark red Carnaby Street polo sweater. Carnaby Street in London's Soho area was probably the most famous sixties shopping venue in the world. London led the way in trendy clothes. I will cover this subject in more detail later, but I still have the sweater.

Girls also tended to dress differently, with tight jumpers, miniskirts and leather boots. We boys did not object to this, particularly when lectures got a bit boring. We could think long about the Saturday disco and whom we might dance with!

One article of clothing which is rarely worn now by students is the university or college scarf. In the sixties, all students wore their scarf and it was one way in which you could pick them out. I still have, somewhere, my UOLU (University of London Union) one.

Today, particularly the girls, they wear designer clothes which were virtually unheard of forty years ago. Pamela tells me she knows girls who spend over three hundred pounds each month on clothes and shoes. How do they afford them? I am sure parental support comes into play, or should I say pay!

Entertainments such as clubs, parties, discos and going to the cinema have changed very little over the last forty years but they have become more sophisticated with modern technology and a huge variety of venues. The COVID-19 virus is unfortunately likely to change all this.

Pamela usually eats out several times a week at the Union, pubs and local restaurants. Back in the sixties, we went out less frequently and the choice was limited unless you went into central London. McDonalds had yet to come to Britain and pub meals were generally rolls, sandwiches and maybe meat pies.

The microwave oven of course had not been invented and there was a limited range of frozen food, particularly in the early 1960s. How different it is today, and also in relative terms much cheaper. The top eatery to us back then was the Angus Steak House where a rump steak with chips and vegetables would cost around five pounds and ten shillings, including a pint of beer. I remember 'Worthington E' beer from the barrel was really good back then!

As mentioned, in those days, my weekly rent including evening meals etc. was around six pounds per week! So in today's money that would equate to a hundred or more. Mars bars were then just 4d (eight pence). Today they are closer to a pound.

I also asked Pamela if she knew any students in lodgings and her reply was, "What are those?" When I explained more, she said, "Oh, we don't have lodgings in our uni at Loughborough," but I am not sure about this!

Freshers' Week at Loughborough also had some 'interesting' events such as the unofficial mixed naked four hundred metre run. The university is recognised as the best one for sport in the UK but not many people in the town know about this particular pastime.

Each new undergraduate now received a freshers' pack including a t-shirt, campus map, 'Hey Ewe' pack (which I shall explain later), a shot glass, hat and a condom (which I shall not explain later).

Technology has transformed modern life now and as a chemistry student I needed to perform complex calculations. Calculators were only just coming onto the market towards the end of my course and we had to therefore rely on 'slide rules'. For those of you who do not know about these, they were originally invented back in 1654 by Robert Bissaker, and following John Napier's development of logarithms, enabled rapid mathematical calculations to be made. Slide rules consisted of two calibrated rules which could move rapidly and produce results. They were used by all scientists and engineers up until the production of the computer in the late 1960s.

I can still do some calculations using a slide rule faster than an electronic calculator and they don't require batteries! Without doubt the introduction of the personal computer and Microsoft has changed the world and altered every facet of our lives today. Calculations which took hours to perform forty years ago can now take microseconds, plus the technology is available to all of us on our home PCs.

It's amazing to think that great engineers like Isambard Kingdom Brunel and Thomas Telford in the 1820s probably did most of their calculations using a slide rule, as indeed did some of the early rocket scientists in America and Russia.

Back in the sixties, communication with home was almost entirely by letter, whereas today's students can email, text or phone on their mobile or even use the phone in each room at their halls of residence. How easy students have it today! Pamela was now starting to communicate with us back home by email. What does concern me, and I know that she is not alone, is the poor quality of punctuation and the shortening of words.

I am sure her generation of text messaging writes in this abbreviated style of using 'U' for you, 'im' for I am, 'r' for are and many more. 'TBH im busy ATM' = To be honest I am busy at the moment! I wondered whether Pamela's lecturers accepted this lack of proper writing in her projects and reports etc.

Monday, week seven – panic call from Pamela: "Some b**** has switched off our freezer over the weekend and we and more importantly I, have lost a week's supply of frozen food plus my fellow student neighbour has been ill with a food problem and to add to my worries I have also cut my finger with a carving knife!" What she was carving I am not quite sure!

I tried to reassure her by saying, "By the way did you have a good weekend?"

Tuesday, week seven – received an amazing phone call from Pamela. She and five other girls were proposing to visit a house tomorrow which they intend to share in year two next October. Such confidence, and how different it is to when she first started at Loughborough back in September for Freshers' Week. Miss Confidence 2005!

I am not sure which is worse: all lads together or all girls? We have always tried to teach Pamela the importance of a tidy room but I have to admit that we have not always been successful and I am sure that most daughters are similar. I would wait with interest to see how organised the girls are when they move in together next year.

In terms of work, this is one area that has not changed as most students still need to work long hours outside lectures to keep on top of their course studies. Pamela tells me that she often works until after midnight to complete projects. However, not all students do this and little has changed since the sixties as there are a few who see university as an opportunity for maximising their social and entertainment time at the expense of studies – year one usually sorts them out!

Relationships have changed with professors and lecturers. In my day they were always referred to as professor, doctor or sir and never by their first name except young PHD students whom we always called by their first names.

Now all of Pamela's lecturers are called Simon or Dave or whatever and whereas we were called by our surname or the few girls on our course by 'Miss…', my daughter is referred to as Pam. There are also a number of lecturers who really think that they are still students and one of the crowd. She is not sure that such familiarity is wise!

Pamela has already been home for a weekend and although by road it takes just fifty minutes, by train it can be over three hours – which works out at just thirteen miles per hour! This involves a train to Leicester then on to Birmingham New Street and finally on to a third local train service on the cross-city line. It probably took me not much more than this to get to London and back in 1965 on the steam train. Surely this is not progress!

One of the problems of coming home is the trauma of going back on the Sunday night, particularly in the depths of winter. It would be interesting to see how Pamela felt after the Christmas break. However she will have the luxury of travelling back by car and this time to friends back at her hall.

In my second year at university I did have my own car, which surprisingly was not all that rare and some students, particularly those from overseas, had better vehicles than some of the lecturers!

My very first car was a ten-year-old Austin A40 Devon, black of course and cost me just twenty-seven pounds and ten shillings. I loved it and called it 'Matilda' because it had poor shock absorbers and would waltz along the road. Of course this was before MOT tests!

University lecturers are not like teachers and little has changed over the years within their sheltered worlds. The same law of life applies: 'those who can do, those who cannot, teach. Those who cannot teach, teach teachers to teach and those who cannot teach teachers to teach, administrate'.

I should like to add one – 'Those who cannot administrate become university lecturers.' However, all are characters who add to life's rich pattern and make university a unique experience for students.

With the end of term one at Loughborough approaching, Pamela attended the John Phillips Christmas Ball at a hotel in Nottingham with some hundred and twenty other students and apart from a few thick heads in the morning, the evening passed without incident.

I do not recall that we had similar events back in the 1960s, other than the annual Rag Ball and the Chemical Society Dinner, the latter being more exciting than you might think!

After eleven weeks completed of term one at Loughborough, I collected Pamela from John Phillips Hall on Saturday morning with more bags and cases etc. than I thought I had originally transported back in September and still she left a cupboard full in her room! She was really looking forward to being driven home for Christmas and the sounds of carols and Christmas music on the car radio added to the occasion. Three weeks at home with mum's cooking and looking after her needs was really appreciated for the first time in her life.

Yes, we were again real parents!

Over Christmas she was also taking an interest in cooking which was becoming a new skill and pastime. Even food shopping was becoming a new experience. I was particularly impressed how she was handling money to ensure that she obtained value on such items. Buying cheap products was not always cost effective!

Whilst Pamela had a temporary job as a waitress in the summer at a local restaurant, she had projects to complete over Christmas and time was not available for her to take on other work.

I remember that when I was a student I had a number of short-term jobs and over many Christmases I worked for the GPO (General Post Office), now Royal Mail, delivering letters. I understand that now, probably due to changes in postmen's shift arrangements, students are no longer employed. I had to get up each morning at around five a.m. and report for duty at the local sorting office. I even had to sign a document, something not dissimilar to the Official Secrets Act, before I signed on. The usual postmen stayed in at the depot and sent the students out into the cold to deliver Christmas cards and parcels.

After a few years I managed eventually to secure a position on handling parcels which was regarded as a cushy number as all deliveries were made by van. There was a shortage of vans and we used an 'ice cream' van, which was very appropriate in the ice and snow. I forgot the number of times we were asked for ice cream cornets by the kids!

One of the pleasures of delivering presents was that many children thought that we were Father Christmas's helper and their parents would often reward us with money or hot mince pies. Surprisingly, it was the poorer houses on the council estates that rewarded us more often.

The range and sizes of letterboxes ranged considerably and particularly at the grand houses they were huge and could easily take vast amounts of mail. Today, most houses have a standardised box which results in several passes when there is a lot of mail.

These were magic times and we also looked forward each day to the first delivery of a bacon sandwich and hot tea back at the sorting office canteen known as 'The Wharf'. I can still remember how good this was.

The regular postmen also enjoyed the company, particularly of the female students over the pre-Christmas period. The girls often stayed over to help with sorting the huge load of mail.

Although hard work, it enabled us students to have extra cash over the festive season. The postmen were also a good source of jokes but few do I remember except this one which was doing the rounds back in 1965.

'One Christmas, a long time ago, Father Christmas was ready for his Christmas run but there were problems, despite the support he was having from the regular postmen. Four of his elves were sick and the trainee elves did not work as fast as the regular ones, so Father Christmas was beginning to fall behind schedule.

Mrs Christmas told Father Christmas that her mother was coming to visit them and that caused him more stress. When he went to harness his reindeer, two had escaped! When he went to load the sleigh, one of the boards cracked and the toy bag fell to the ground and scattered all the toys.

Father Christmas went into the house for a cup of coffee with a large nip of whisky. When he went to the cupboard, he discovered that the elves had hidden the whisky and there was nothing to drink!

In his frustration he dropped the coffee pot and it smashed all over the floor. He was at the end of his tether when the doorbell rang… When he opened the door there was an angel with a large Christmas tree!

The angel said cheerfully, "Merry Christmas, Father Christmas. Where would you like me to put this tree?"

And so the tradition of the angel on top of the Christmas tree began!

Chapter 3 – Year 1, Term 2

With the New Year came term two and the beginning of the real British winter. With the car packed to the brim again, with even more luggage than before Christmas, we proceeded to drive back to Loughborough. I was beginning to think that I would need to hire a van when I collected her at the end of the summer term! I also wondered how students manage who go to university in, say, Aberdeen or Belfast? Surely they have to travel light?

Pamela appeared to be a lot more confident in her second term and we felt that she had already learnt some valuable lessons about life. She still could not resist buying items of clothing in the January sales, but I am sure that she is not alone. We also had to provide her with a new computer printer with copying and scanning facilities.

A few years ago, this would have cost a fortune but we only paid £49.99 at the local PC store. Amazing! The catch of course is that the replacement ink cartridges cost nearly as much as the printer!

So after dropping her off at the John Phillips Hall, I then returned home to just my wife. We had already adapted to Pamela being with us over Christmas – would we ever get used to these regular changes?

The spring term was just ten weeks and then back home for four weeks before the final term of year one. How quickly the time was passing!

Back at Loughborough, the students' busy social life began again with the usual weekly events at the Union:

Sunday: Big Quiz Night with cash prizes and cheap drinks

Monday: Champagne evening with a DJ and Champagne/ Red Bull

Tuesday: 'Cheezy Tuesday' with 'breakdance' battles and a crazy atmosphere

Wednesday: Hey Ewe (originally AU, Athletic Union) with pop classics and again cheap drinks and 'totty spotting'

Thursday: Band Night

Friday: FND (Friday night disco) with five rooms to satisfy any musical taste

Saturday: Comedy Night (which actually finishes at ten p.m.!)

I understood that Pamela did not attend every night but always on Wednesdays and had been spotted and photographed as 'totty' material. What do I say?

After much pressure, Pamela now has a TV licence, as do her friends in 'Cell Block H'. With so much pressure on students to handle their finances, it seems unreasonable that they each have to fork out £126.50 just for having a portable TV set! Not all students do, but they risk a thousand pound fine if caught.

I remember my son telling me that when he was at uni some five years before, when the detector van was spotted on campus, each hall phoned the next one so that TVs could be hidden and they would sit in the kitchen until the threat had passed.

I had better not mention which university he attended, as I am sure the practice still goes on. When I was a student, portable TVs did not exist but we did have access to an ancient black and white set which worked on a good day but the picture was poor.

We particularly rushed back home to watch Top of The Pops and The Magic Roundabout, the latter of which was also surprisingly popular with many of our lecturers.

Top of the Pops in the early days had shots of the girls' legs and beyond with the cameramen lying on the studio floor – very popular with boys like ourselves! Still, it was the Swinging Sixties. Of course we poor students had a TV licence! I cannot remember there being a detector van back in the 1960s – perhaps they had not been invented?

As term two progressed, Pamela's confidence continued to grow and she was enjoying the experience with her new-found friends.

Her room had also been transformed from a sparse cell into a cosy student pad with posters, photographs and subtle lighting. You could tell she was an art and graphics student.

In late January, she phoned one evening to say that she had passed her first assessment and was very pleased as indeed we were. Unfortunately some of her group were not so lucky and would have to retake it in the summer and pay for the privilege. Also she had heard that her essay on the Birmingham Bullring had been marked a 2:1 – which I understand is good!

Pamela's student loan had now reached over two thousand, eight hundred pounds but she was managing her money well and I was impressed with her prudence.

She was also lining up work for the summer vacation, after which she would be in a house-share with five other girls. Some students had spent the loan in the first few weeks and I even heard of one girl who spent the entire amount having breast implants at a private clinic.

Although Pamela was enjoying university life, coming home every other weekend was becoming routine practice with most of her friends. Maybe this would change in year two?

Back in the 1960s when I was in London, I probably came home just once a term, mainly for birthdays and special occasions. However it was always difficult when the time came to go back, and even after three years I still had not fully come to terms with this, particularly in the winter. After forty years, I can still remember the heartfelt goodbyes – but it did make me a stronger person. Many people who have never left home miss out on this.

Pamela had registered with a local doctor on campus. As a child, she had never really liked going to the doctor and when she had an allergic reaction on her hand from using inks, my advice was to arrange an appointment. However, despite the red rash itching on her left hand (and she is left-handed), she preferred to borrow some hydrocortisone cream from one of her friends – a rugby-playing student on her floor. But after a few days it did start to get better.

During my student days in London, I never once visited a doctor but particularly in my final year when I shared a house with two other students I might have had a good reason. At the bottom of the garden of our rented house in Eltham, South East London, was a graveyard and the nearest doctor's house backed onto this graveyard. His name was Dr H. J. Blood.

Now, before becoming an undergraduate I was very sceptical about anything to do with the paranormal, but when I left London my mind was changed by several spooky experiences which I shall explain in a later chapter.

With five weeks left of term two back at 'Cell Block H', Pamela's kitchen on her floor was already in a disgusting state and urgent action was needed. Her friend (a rugby player) came to the rescue and spent long hours cleaning every surface until they all shone. For his reward, their floor won the 'Hall Kitchen of the Week' award, which offered both money off and food vouchers at the Union.

Could they maintain this standard? Pamela was hopeful and proceeded to strategically place notices for users to please leave the place as they found it, 'in a clean state at all times'. Perhaps pressure was needed to enforce this request. Bring in the kitchen police!

It is also interesting to note how the perception of students has changed over the years. Loughborough is a small town in Leicestershire and the student population far exceeds the other residents, although many rely on the university for work. But do the 'workers' really like the students? For most the answer is probably no. Some are obviously frustrated, like the announcer at Loughborough Rail Station who, prior to the arrival of a train, said, "I am sure nobody is listening to me but the next train to arrive will be to Leicester City and I hope that all you students travelling pay more attention to your lectures than you do to me."

In the sixties, although students were starting to be recognised, most universities were very cloistered environments and cut off from the real world. This particularly applied to 'red brick' universities with large campuses.

I wore a tie, as did most of my male friends, to attend lectures and it was only a few who appeared to rebel and follow the protest movements and listen to the sounds of people like Bob Dylan, Joan Baez and others. America was still at war with Vietnam and worldwide, students were against the proliferation of US war policies.

Demonstrations were common in Central London outside the American Embassy. Today of course we still have wars in Iraq, Syria and Afghanistan – little has changed!

One area where students have an impact on the local environment is Rag Week and ongoing fund-raising activities. Loughborough, I understand, raised over seven hundred thousand pounds for charities last year, making the university number one in the UK for the amount of money donated to charities.

Now for a bit of nostalgia, looking back to events in the decade of the 1960s.

1960 – Birth of the Austin Mini car and also the youngest ever and first Roman Catholic president of the USA was to be John Fitzgerald Kennedy.

1961 – Russian cosmonaut Yuri Gagarin became the first man to orbit the Earth in Vostok 1 and the Berlin Wall was built.

What amazing events!

1962 – John Glenn orbited the Earth on Friendship 7, part of Project Mercury. The Cuban missile crisis began. Marilyn Monroe died. The first episode of Steptoe and Son was shown.

1963 – Telstar was launched, enabling transatlantic communication by satellite. On November 22nd, President Kennedy was assassinated in Dallas, Texas.

1964 – The first screening of Dr Who and the launch of BBC2, giving a choice of three channels.

1965 – Sir Winston Churchill died. Cigarette advertising was banned and a new maximum speed on our few motorways of seventy miles per hour was introduced. Jeremy Fell left home for university in London by way of the new M1 motorway.

1966 – England wins the World Cup, beating West Germany. The Aberfan disaster struck South Wales and killed over one hundred children.

1967 – The breathalyser was introduced by Barbara Castle, Minister for Transport. 'Wonderful Radio One' also launched in September.

1968 – Martin Luther King was killed. Apollo 8 orbited the moon on Christmas Day and the astronauts read extracts from the Bible.

1969 – The halfpenny piece ceased to be legal currency and Prince Charles was crowned the Prince of Wales. Full colour television came to BBC1. Concord's first supersonic test flight happened and Apollo 11 landed on the Moon with humankind's first walk on its surface. The day before, a cancelled TV show from America began on BBC1 – its name: 'Star Trek'!

What an amazing decade the sixties was and we also saw the screening of James Bond films, the 'flower power' movement and the Swinging Sixties in the pop world.

Back to the present – three weeks to go before the end of term and all the university lecturers are on strike over pay.

I cannot remember this happening when I was at university but the sixties were a time of workers on strike almost every day, particularly in the motor trade.

The shop steward for British Leyland, who made the Mini (subsequently Austin Rover), was known as 'Red Robbo' and constantly at war with the management, headed by a Canadian, Michael Edwardes.

The media covered many strikes during this period and it looked at the time as if the disruption would never end – British Leyland in Birmingham and Oxford, Ford at Dagenham and Vauxhall in Halewood and other sites. The quality of the cars was very poor and I remember my first new Ford Escort, the wings of which had rusted through in just twelve months. Before this, I had a Triumph Herald which was much better quality and even had a sunshine roof.

On Monday morning in the second week of March I woke up feeling really well and looking forward to a busy but productive time. By late afternoon, I had a severe sore throat, headache and the feeling that I was due for my first head cold in five years – and yes, Pamela had similar symptoms when she came back for the weekend.

I was at death's door and needed the utmost sympathy! Two days later I was on the mend, helped by generous helpings of whisky – for medicinal reasons of course! However, I was left with such a deep voice that few people would recognise me.

An opportunity, I thought, to have some fun? So I phoned Pamela on her room phone and the conversation went like this: "Good morning. This is the vice chancellor's office and my name is Colin Montgomery. I am contacting you and a number of students at John Phillips Hall regarding the heating arrangement. Is that Miss Pamela Fell on floor two, Block H?"

"Yes," she said, wondering what I was going to ask.

I replied, "As you may be aware, gas and electricity prices are increasing rapidly and having discussed the position with the university bursar this morning we are considering switching off heating during the daytime hours. Would this cause a problem for you, Miss Fell?"

She answered, not realising it was her dad, saying "Probably not," so I added that we were also looking for students only having a shower every other week and would this be OK? The line went dead, although I was going to suggest that further savings could be made by sharing showers with fellow students. Perhaps just as well I did not take it to the next stage! Later I explained that it was just a bit of fun but Pamela did not see it that way!

Back in the sixties, a friend of mine worked for a government department in Birmingham city centre on the fifth floor of an office block and he had a colleague who liked to 'wind people up' and play practical jokes. He was appropriately nicknamed 'Crank'!

I recall one of his acts was that he noticed that the telephone box in view of his office window always had the light on, so he found the number and waited until he saw an unsuspecting person passing by and then phoned. The conversation went like this: "Hello, this is the GPO here. May I please ask you a favour? The light in this box has been left on so could you please switch it off by the floor?"

Crank watched as the unfortunate 'candidate' got down on his knees to find the switch, which of course was not there. On speaking back to him, Crank explained that this was obviously a D92 B model unit and the only way to switch the light off was to go to the outside of the box and gently tap on the rear – which the person usually did, to no avail.

Later he spoke with the man, or often woman; Crank then said this has been a windup and they were filming for a new TV show, but if they crossed the road and went into the post office they could claim their fifty pound reward; of course there was none. This must have really annoyed the staff!

Other pranks included writing to companies such as Oak Insurance asking if he could insure the tree in his garden, plus Tulip Hire, who specialised in heavy mechanical plant hire and asked, as his daughter was getting married soon, if he could hire tulips for the reception.

Amazingly he often received replies. The last I heard of him was that he was paid by the News of The World newspaper for his article on being a public nuisance. I wonder where he is now?

Back in Loughborough, it was the end of term party 'Boogie Night' for just five pounds each with special guests the Foundations. Would you ever believe that forty years ago this same 'group', as it was known back then, performed at our end of term event? Amazing!

I cannot remember what the cost was but it was probably not around five pounds. Some of you older readers might remember their top ten hit 'Build Me Up Buttercup' and yes, they played it again. Makes me feel young!

Now with the end of term it was back home for Pamela for the Easter holidays and four weeks of being looked after.

Just before Easter, as a special treat, we decided to take Pamela to Paris and show her around some of the many museums and places of interest.

The flight from Birmingham took off on time and it touched down at Charles De Gaulle Airport in just fifty-five minutes. Then followed fifteen minutes for the aircraft to reach its parking area, five minutes by airport coach to Terminal 2 Arrivals and then some forty-five minutes to clear customs and wait for the Air France coach to central Paris – by which time we were 'travel worn'.

But there was more to come!

This journey to the centre took about fifty minutes via the infamous 'peripherique': Paris's answer to the M25. In all, three and a half hours plus a further one and a half hours at the departure lounge at Birmingham waiting for the flight. Back in the early 1970s, I did a similar trip, travelling on British European Airways by turbo-jet aircraft in less than two and a half hours. Have we really progressed?

The sun was shining in Paris and unlike England in April, we were able to sit at a pavement cafe and watch the world go by. The city still has a lot to offer and the musée de Louvre was huge and I believe it is the largest museum in the world.

It's famous of course for Leonardo's Mona Lisa and the Venus de Milo. It was very impressive and contains more than three hundred and fifty thousand priceless objects. Many of the paintings were looted from Italy in the sixteenth century which no doubt still displeases Italians.

Pamela was particularly impressed by the glass pyramid entrance, designed by a Monsieur I.M. Pei in 1989. It is unique and famous throughout the world.

Of course, no trip to Paris would be complete for Pamela without some serious retail therapy and Galeries Lafayette in Boulevard Haussmann was the closest that she had been to shopping heaven. In fact, she could have easily stayed there all day but we had to prise her away after the purchase of two skirts and a top!

On Sunday, we took a lunch cruise on the Bateaux Mouches, starting at the foot of the Eiffel Tower along the River Seine. The views were spectacular and the food/wine excellent – as is always in France. The short break had done us all good but the time was soon approaching to travel back to the UK via the huge queues of Charles De Gaulle Airport.

Terminal 2 needed rebuilding and to be better organised – it was a mess! It gave the wrong impression to travellers entering the French capital city. They would learn a lot from Birmingham International Airport which I think is among the best in the world! Perhaps I am biased, but within five minutes of landing we were in a taxi on our way home.

During the Easter break, Pamela worked really hard on a number of graphic design projects. In the past, I felt that arts undergraduates worked fewer hours than their counterparts in science and engineering but I have to admit that with her degree course there is little spare time.

Again the time had come to take Pamela back to uni in Loughborough for the final term of year one – how quickly the time had passed!

Shortly before dropping her back at cell block H, we called at Sainsbury's in Loughborough where we noticed the same phenomenon as in the restaurant when we first took her prior to Freshers' Week.

Throughout the supermarket on Sunday afternoon there were groups of three people shopping – students with their mums and dads loading their purchases into trolleys for the new term.

I wondered whether they were going back to that Loughborough restaurant and asking for 'a table for three please'!

Chapter 4 – Year 1, Term 3

Back at Loughborough, the new term did not start well for Pamela. Firstly her central heating was stuck on high and even with the window open it was still very hot. One of her neighbours on the floor below was playing his music until the early hours and she could not sleep. The next day, her year were informed that as the design studio was being redecorated, they need not come in and she could have had a few extra days at home.

Since September, Pamela had made many new friends and she was well liked by most students with a few exceptions – namely Jeff, a plump gentlemen who was affectionately known as 'Dank'. He lived exactly under her room at John Phillips Court on the floor below and often played his music loudly into the early hours of the morning.

Despite requests, he refused to turn it down so in desperation she poured a cup or two of water from her window onto his towels left out to dry over the sill. This did not please Dank, so the dispute went on! The lack of sleep was stressing her out, so further action was required.

The pressure on Pamela to complete projects and essays on time was more noticeable as the end of her first year approached. Unlike other courses, graphic communications was one of continuous assessment rather than examinations. Working long hours resulted in a series of minor medical problems which she put down to stress. Living in a close community also results in any infections being passed on to one another. Several students had coughs and colds which were difficult to clear, even with antibiotics.

All students have a certain amount of stress, and back in the 1960s it was no different but the goal of obtaining a degree outweighed the problems. However, some people could not cope and it was sad to see them drop out – usually in the first year. The only real time I felt stressed was at the end of each year's exams, particularly in the third year. I realised that these final exams were critical and would alter the path of my life. The results I shall detail later.

Back at Loughborough, it was the Summer Ball at a hotel in Leicester with Pamela and her friends looking forward to the evening. However, there were problems! Unfortunately a number of gatecrashers boarded the coaches and when Pamela and her friend arrived, they were told that there were no places for them on their hall's table so they ended up on another table where they knew no one. When they complained, they were advised that the organisers had forgotten to bring the table plan with them. What a way to organise such an event! The food was also poor, no water was on the tables, drinks took an age to be served and she felt the twenty-eight-pound ticket price was not justified.

The problem with 'Dank' and his late-night music continued and she had learnt that he often went out and just left his CD player on. She had therefore given up any hope of sorting out the problem as there was only less than two weeks before the end of the term.

Generally this third term had not been a great one and she was looking forward to her friends all sharing a house in year two.

Pamela's academic performance, since she passed her GCSEs with many A-stars and four good 'A' levels plus her foundation art qualification, had been impressive. She had never failed any examination and at Loughborough the first two terms followed the same pattern. However, in late May we received a panic phone call saying she was so upset she couldn't talk! Apparently she had failed her drawing module and she would have to retake the assignment in August. If she failed again she would be out of the university! Shock horror!

We therefore tried to console her and I mentioned my own view of people who apparently sail through their life without some setbacks. My experience has been that eventually they fail. In a carefully worded email, I said to her: 'Imagine if say several years ahead you're working for a large PR/design agency and have spent huge amounts of time on a project when the graphics director calls you in and says, "Pamela, this is rubbish; we can't use it." Only by having experience of perceived failure can you address such issues. We have all gone through similar problems.

'I too failed my second year at university in London but I was spurred on to reach final success – and look what I have achieved in my career! Not many people have been at the top of their profession like me!

'The painter John Constable was a perceived failure in the UK and only when his work became popular in France did he gain recognition in England. He suffered from much stress in his earlier days as an artist but few painters in the world have matched his talent, with his pictures now selling for millions of pounds.

'History confirms that many people who were once regarded as failures recognised the fact and moved on to be highly successful – not just in their chosen profession!

'We are fully behind you so dust yourself off and tell them that you WILL succeed! You have not let us down and we are confident you will gain your BA and go on to higher things. As I keep saying, your talent is in your ideas and this will see you through – believe me.'

Later that week she felt more comfortable about the position. Amazingly, having just spoken about her talents, Pamela was staging an end of term show of her graphic design work along with other students at a local hotel. Here she was approached by a gentleman from a major wrapping paper company and he was impressed with several of her designs and suggested that she emailed copies to him for consideration. If accepted, she would receive a fee for her artwork. She was very excited about this opportunity and spent the last weekend before she finished year one preparing the details.

The third Friday in June was here and after eight months I was on the road to collect Pamela for the summer break. How quickly Pamela's first year had gone and now we had to get used to her being back home for four months! My car was outside 'Cell Block H' being loaded up for the last time and it was touch and go as to whether we could find enough space for the range of cases and bags accumulated over the year.

She had made many new friends and several hugged her prior to our departure and plans were in hand to meet again during the holidays.

Back at home, Pamela's thoughts turned to her holiday job back as a waitress at the cafe in our local garden centre, a job she had the previous summer. Most of her friends were unable to obtain temporary work during the vacation so she felt herself lucky. The job paid the minimum wage but the conditions were pleasant and the staff were friendly.

When I was a student there were more choices in the summer months, although some of my jobs were, to say the least, undesirable and included:

– Painting white lines in the middle of roads for the borough council. This gave me real power over the traffic and diverting vehicles. The plus point was many tea breaks and often we students were left for hours without supervision: a situation which would not happen now with health and safety legislation. Some, not me of course, took advantage of the situation.

– Working in a darkroom of a photo lab printing people's holiday snaps. This meant that I did not see daylight during working hours. We also got to see some 'interesting' holiday photographs. I'll leave it to your imagination what they were!

– A gardener at the local crematorium. My colleagues who worked there were a strange bunch and I had a number of unusual memories of things that happened, some of which I shall detail later.

– Working as a DIY products salesman at a departmental store in Birmingham called Lewis's – low pay and long hours! I did get a discount on selected purchases though!

Back to the crematorium. Although I worked in the gardens, our coffee and lunch breaks were taken in the mess in the main block behind the four gas-fired cremators. Many people think that after the funerals the corpses are taken out of the coffins but the reality is that all is burnt. Gas ignition was automatic and once up to temperature, about one thousand, five hundred degrees Celsius, the process could be completed in less than an hour.

A particularly spooky story is that each cremator chamber had to be cleaned on a regular basis with a wire brush. The procedure was that the operative had to open both the front and rear cremator doors and work backwards, removing the soot deposits. However, when reaching the end, the operative had to close the front door situated behind the chapel area and walk right round the building back to the other door.

To save time, one assistant had a habit of closing the door in front of him and working backwards. On one occasion, the cleaner in the public chapel area accidentally closed the front door to the cremator and when he reached the end the poor chap was locked in. He knew that within minutes, the ignition would come on automatically.

The unfortunate operative was therefore banging frantically on the door but most people were out of the building. By strange coincidence, the manager of the crematorium had left some papers in his office and returned to collect them and heard the banging. Thus the man was released from his potential nightmare scenario with just minutes to spare! Needless to say, he never closed another cremator door again!

Pamela's summer holidays were passing quickly with part-time working as a waitress and completion of her graphic design assignment which had to be handed in at Loughborough by 25th August.

It was looking good and she had come up with a number of novel ideas to depict the three modules of 'home', 'flying' and 'tops' using various media. This entailed eighty drawings. I even lay awake at night thinking of how she could illustrate these topics but she had plenty of her own ideas which I had to admit looked very good when produced on paper.

Finally, after over a hundred and twenty hours of work, the project was completed and I drove her to Loughborough to hand the final work in to the university offices.

Her drawing, which she hoped would gain her a place in the second year, was a map-shaped heart of the Birmingham area on a larger shape of Great Britain with the words 'Home is where the heart is', which I thought looked really professional. She anticipated the result in late September. All fingers were crossed!

As mid-August approached, Pamela's last day as a waitress at the garden centre passed without incident but her thoughts were focused on the results of her project and despite our reassurances she felt pessimistic as to her future.

It was quite simple; if she failed to get over forty per cent for her drawing module, her studies at the university would be terminated. As 'D-Day' arrived, she nervously phoned the office to receive the result which was advised as being a pass with marks over forty-eight per cent.

She was, to say the least, very relieved and she could now look forward to year two with confidence. To celebrate she went on a clothes shopping spree! More tops and handbags to take back?

Unfortunately, several of her fellow students had failed to achieve a pass which meant she probably would not see them again, although they could repeat the year. I often thought as a chemistry undergraduate that art students had an easy ride but perhaps I underestimated their studies. Obviously in such a competitive area as graphics it was only the best students that went forward.

Pamela was also working on a presentation of a graphic stage set which had to be made in early October to her lecturers and fellow students. Her chosen subject was the Crufts dog show which she had picked from a list including such topics as crown green bowling, Polynesian tattoos, Joseph Wedgwood, the Pony Club and morris dancing.

Her idea was to have her face painted with ears to resemble a dog and make her presentation from a kennel perched on top of a table – and of course Dad was commissioned to build such a construction out of lightweight materials (as it and all her belongings had shortly to be transported to her house for the beginning of year two).

I had to admit that the final kennel looked really good with its red roof and brown wood-like sides – plus I rather enjoyed the task. I had worked out a way in which it could be flat packed and easily assembled. IKEA would have been proud of me.

Pamela's year at Loughborough had been quite an experience but I think she had learned a lot about herself and life. You win some and lose some!

I think that I also learnt a lot about life in my first year away from home in the 1960s.

So ended year one of university for Pamela.

Chapter 5 – Year 2, Term 1

Almost the start of year two at Loughborough University and although twelve months seemed a long time ago, strangely it had passed very quickly. Unfortunately, due to an injury to my knee I was unable to drive and my son Simon stepped in to take his sister back. To say the least, we only just managed to get all her items in his car and there was even more luggage than last year's trip. She also had several new possessions including an iPod docking station which of course now made her CD/radio player obsolete.

Her housemates were to share a house in Loughborough and Pamela had secured the largest room, which was situated on the second floor of a mid-terraced house. With Simon having the latest mobile phone with 'Bluetooth', he was able to show us a short video of the property on his return from taking her back. It looked really good and a big improvement on 'Cell Block H' of last year. She would also be rid of Dank playing his music day and night.

It would be interesting to see how she got on with her friends over the next year, as seeing them every day is very different to meeting for just social events.

It is obvious that most young people today strive to have the latest technology, which simply didn't exist when I was their age. Whether they are any happier remains to be seen. Back in 1968, I too moved into a shared house with two of my friends and we had a great time together. The house had no central heating and we simply sat around an electric fire in the small room off the scullery/kitchen and froze when we went to bed at night. In the winter, can you believe, we used to have ice on the inside of the windows!

Pamela's house is close to both a chip shop and a pub. We too had the White Lion pub down the road from our London house. Particularly on a Friday night, we used to leave our home and run as fast as possible to the bar with the last one to arrive buying the first round of drinks. We were always out of breath and could hardly speak and I bet the barman thought we were chronic asthmatics!

Also to start with we had an elderly lady, Mrs Gregory, as a tenant on the first floor of the house but she eventually moved on, I suspect because of the noises we students were making. Had I been in her position, I would have complained to the landlord so we were embarrassed when she finally said she was leaving.

The house, as mentioned in chapter one, I still believe today was haunted. Also the house was always chilly even with several electric fires on. One evening, we met some Swedish au pair girls at the pub and invited them back for coffee. Someone suggested that we have a seance and play ouija board with an upturned glass and the letters of the alphabet in a circle. "Is there a spirit in the room?" we asked and the glass moved to 'yes'. "What is your name?" And the glass moved and spelled out 'Kerschoft'. Strange, but we decided to stop the game.

My bedroom was on the ground floor at the back of the house and was the previous owner's study; it always smelt of cigars. Around three a.m. that night I was awoken by a cold sensation and without a word of a lie, I saw and smelt cigar smoke drifting across the room. I froze! It was a very frightening experience and I tried to sleep the rest of the night with the light on. The occurrence never happened again but the house remained cold.

Several weeks later, we were talking to our landlord and asked, who was the previous owner of the house?

He replied that it was an antiquarian bookseller, a 'Mr Kerschoft' who had originally come from Austria. He had died the year before – and yes, he was a chain cigar smoker! I went cold and from that day on I have believed that there are forces which we do not understand.

They say the spirits often associate themselves with young people and children. We had another experience when on holiday in France some eight years ago when we rented a house in a small hamlet in Brittany called Moëlan-sur-Mer. The house was a typical Breton building with a pretty rose garden on the front. Although it was mid-summer with temperatures around thirty degrees Celsius, the inside of the house was always cool.

My wife and I had a ground floor bedroom overlooking the rear gardens and Pamela (who was twelve at the time) had the first floor bedroom.

On entering the house, Pamela said that the other bedroom at the front did not feel right. It was obviously a young girl's room, with posters of French pop stars, probably from the 1960s and also a large straw hat on the wall. She said she would not sleep in this room so she opted for the third bedroom next to another room which was locked.

The owner of the property was a middle-aged French woman who spoke no English. Many French people often rent out their houses for the summer and stay in a smaller house or flat until they move back for the winter.

The first incident occurred on the second day when I noticed a blonde lock of hair on the landing carpet by the bathroom. All of our family have dark hair so where and how had it fallen to the floor? My wife Judith had also complained of a cool breeze in our bedroom even with the windows closed.

In the relatively large dining room, there was a locked glass china cabinet, on top of which was a flowery photograph dedicated to a young girl who had died a few years ago. Under this was a short note in French which I roughly translated as saying:

'Dedicated to Pascale, who was tragically taken away from us so young and sadly missed by all who knew her. Her spirit lives on in the air of the Cote, the sands, rocks on the beach, and the waters of the sea…'

We suspect that many rooms in the house we had rented were just left, like the girl's bedroom, as they were when Pascale was alive.

Now comes the spooky part, which I really can't rationally explain. On our return to England, Pamela had her 35 mm film developed at the local Boots as she had taken many photographs on the beach, in the garden and around the house. All came out except those taken inside which were blank and not just fogged.

However, there was one exception! A photo of the open entrance door, which showed an apparent green glow emanating from inside. It was very strange because if there was a problem with the camera then surely none of the film would have been developed or printed. I still have that photo somewhere!

It was not one of our best holidays and we certainly would not wish to visit that house again.

We have not had any similar experiences again but since I was young I have always had a special sense or feeling when entering a house as to whether it is a happy or sad home. I am sure that this ability is far from unique with many people.

Back at Loughborough with the start of the new term, Pam was settling in well in her new house and we felt pleased that she sounded so much happier when she phoned home.

On the first Friday, she made her presentation on the Crufts dog show from her kennel perched on top of a desk with her 'dog-like' face paint.

The audience of around fifty fellow students and lecturers applauded her and she felt that it went well – of course having a dad who produced this wonderful kennel must have helped! However, Pam's greatest talent is her ideas which she had demonstrated yet again. We looked forward to seeing the photos!

I often wondered whether in future Pam will use her degree and stay in graphic design or chose a different career.

With my chemistry degree, although I did start off in the chemical industry, my career ended as a director and senior manager at the head office of a major high street bank. However, I have also subsequently performed some consultancy work for a wide range of blue-chip organisations.

Perhaps I could write another book: 'A Chemist at the Bank'? As mentioned, I still firmly believe that the main benefit of going to university is that it demonstrates that you are capable of learning and can live and work independently.

Week two of the new term and all was going well at Loughborough until we had a distraught phone call from Pamela. At eight a.m. that day, workmen had arrived at the house, without any warning, to rewire the electric cables to the whole building. This would take several days. All carpets and floor boards would need to be raised and there would be no lights available. Panic!

The question the six girls asked and also me when I spoke to the letting agent, a guy called Pete, was, "Why was this work not carried out in the summer?"

His answer, which also amazed me, was, "You can't get electricians in the summer months in Loughborough." Perhaps we really do need more Eastern European tradespeople here in England.

The girls were currently paying around fifteen thousand pounds per annum for renting this small terraced house. Perhaps I was in the wrong profession and should have been a landlord but I was determined to sort out the girls' problem.

Pete did not lose his cool, despite my words of concern – he must have been well trained!

He even phoned me later to apologise for the poor handling of the job and did say that my daughter and five of her housemates had visited him this morning to complain. Poor guy!

It's almost like history repeating itself as I had a not dissimilar problem back in 1967 in a small bedsit in Blackheath, South London. Unlike Pam, I was a sole tenant on my own in a strange house. Those of a similar age to me might perhaps remember a 'rogue landlord' by the name of Rachman – mine I am sure was his cousin.

He rented property all over London at extortionate rents because accommodation was very limited. I recall he eventually went to prison for his strong-arm tactics.

My room, if you can call it that, was about ten foot by eight foot with a single bed and a minuscule electric ring and an equally small oven which I can only describe as a plate warmer. The floor was covered in a very cold lino on which I added a small rug to provide some comfort. Several tenants shared a rundown bathroom with a coin-in-the-slot operated Ascot gas heater. The accommodation was all I could afford as a student.

Pam would be staggered if she realised how bad this was and I can imagine prisoners in our jails today having better conditions. Worse was yet to come as in early October of that year, rainwater started pouring down the walls of my room in the early hours of one morning. Unlike now, the early autumn days were really cold and I was so upset that I could easily have come home there and then.

On inspection of the loft area above my second floor accommodation, what I saw took my breath away. There was a large hole in the ancient slate tiled roof which had become home to several families of pigeons – I could not describe the smell.

My heart sank! So that morning, I walked across the frost-covered Blackheath Common to visit the letting agent, Messrs O'Donnell Properties, and waited in a posh reception area. Eventually I spoke to a very well-dressed and well-spoken young lady who took my details and promised that action would be taken.

Despite several calls over the next few days, nothing happened and I left my room. To this day I never got my deposit back, the amount of which I recall was twenty-five pounds – a lot of money in those days.

Following this episode, for the next few weeks I stayed in a local hotel in Blackheath.

It was only after I left to move into my shared house with two other students did I realise the owner of the hotel was Mr O'Donnell – yes the bedsit owner's brother!

How can these people sleep well at night?

Shortly after the new wiring had been completed in the girls' house, their microwave oven gave up the ghost and they purchased another one for just thirty pounds.

By strange coincidence, when Pam came home for the first weekend after six weeks at Loughborough, our two-year-old microwave also stopped working so we ended up buying another one for just £49.99 which also had a convection oven and a grill facility. Amazing! How I would have loved such an item in my bedsit in London.

I remember when we first bought a microwave oven some fifteen years before and it cost three hundred and forty pounds and still works – although I keep it as a spare in our loft. The first domestic microwave ovens I understand were produced in 1969.

Today the major topic in the press is global warming and the environmental issues, which just did not exist in the 1960s, although I do remember analysts predicting that oil and gas supplies would run out by early 2000. How they were wrong!

Today you also hear very little mention of why most white goods such as ovens, refrigerators, washing machines and other electrical items are just not built to last. What a waste of the world's finite materials, let alone energy supplies in their manufacture.

Most suppliers nowadays seem more interested in selling you insurance than having goods which will last. Something has to change in our throwaway society.

Back in Loughborough, the winter term was passing quickly and Pam was becoming more confident. Apparently she rarely now went to events such as 'Hey Ewe' and 'Cheezey Tuesday' nights at the Union. "Those are for freshers and first years," she commented.

In February next year, she would be spending a week in New York, visiting art galleries and other sights of interest to budding graphic designers. In my day as a chemistry student we were lucky to visit an industrial laboratory in London. However, some of my fellow students did spend their work experience in Switzerland with organisations such as Roche and other big pharmaceutical companies.

My industrial experience was gained in a company called Albright and Wilson based in a Black Country town in the West Midlands by the name of Oldbury.

Their main product was phosphorus, which went into many items such as detergents, coatings, fertilisers and even bombs. I worked in the research laboratory and despite the serious nature of what we did, we also had a lot of fun.

One day a colleague bent down to get items from his cupboard below. Suddenly there was an almighty explosion when the heavy, cast iron oven door blew off and travelled with great speed above his head and straight through a cavity wall. The whole building shuddered as no doubt so did he! Thankfully he was not injured.

I also did some work on nuclear magnetic resonance spectroscopy (NMRS) which I will not go into detail about now but it did lead to the development of MRI scanning technology which is now used by hospitals throughout the world. Not many people know that!

With so much discussion about the environment today and global warming, this is not my view, particularly as the former national chairman of the Energy and the Environmental Committee of the Major Energy Users' Council based in London. Some of my comments I expressed at a meeting back in 1987 at a committee that I had the privilege to chair at the House of Lords:

" Yes, the world has a problem with climate change and the reduction of the polar icecaps as the world becomes warmer. The United Kingdom has a major part to play but only as an example to other countries. We need to put this into context as we are but a small nation compared with North and South America, Russia, China and India plus many developing countries which have much larger contributions to make. I feel that if they do not recognise this then life on our planet may change – for better or worse, a fact that I am not totally sure about.

"When I was a young chemist in the early 1970s, we were advised by the media that oil and gas would run out by the end of the century – but it has not happened.

"What really concerns me is that we are using up the world's finite resources such as oil, gas and minerals. Why burn fossil fuels which cannot be replaced? Why have cars and consumer goods which only last a few years and end up in a landfill site?

"In the last ten million years there have been huge changes in the environment and climate. One catastrophic event like the natural explosion of the volcanic island of Krakatoa in 1883 had more power than the total world's arsenal of nuclear bombs.

"Remember the scares about the effects of the nuclear meltdown at Chernobyl in 1986? We are still here and few have suffered any consequences – ladies and gentlemen we must have faith in our futures."

My view of the environment has not changed today but has different aspects to that of the current government. We therefore must be sure that recycling is cost and environmentally effective. Why, for example, drive a four-by-four 'Chelsea tractor' to the bottle bank?

What does actually happen to the refuse which we diligently place in our recycling boxes? I also think that more research is needed into the effects of aircraft pollution in the higher atmosphere, as surely this is one area where the polluter must be held responsible. Again, how is the cost effectiveness measured?

When I was at my first school, my mother would take me on the back of her bike some three miles either way, twice a day, despite the fact that we had a car, which was rare in the 1950s. Today, mothers seem to drive their children to school even if it's a few hundred yards from home. What a waste of fuel, let alone not allowing children to have some exercise.

As mentioned, without doubt my number one concern, which is not being addressed, is that of white consumer goods such as cookers, fridges, washing machines plus televisions and other electrical items which last for just a few years. As mentioned earlier, what a huge waste of the Earth's finite resources, including energy!

Back in the 1960s I don't think I ever heard of the word 'environment'. Household rubbish was usually just put into the bin and never seen again. Dustbins were made of galvanised steel and about half the size of today's plastic wheelie bins. Packaging was in the main paper and cardboard, although polythene bags were just starting to replace them.

When you purchased electrical goods, they would probably come in a cardboard box as polystyrene had yet to be used on a large scale. Perhaps this is one of the reasons why we had smaller bins.

Based on the theory that everything goes round in a circle, will we move back to having less packaging waste and materials? The packaging industry was still in its infancy in the sixties and who would have predicted how huge it is today? Still, it does provide a lot of work for graphic designers!

Yesterday we took our old microwave oven to the municipal tip and I was staggered by the degree of separation of refuse such as televisions, wood, metals, glass, clothing, plastic products, building materials, paper, garden rubbish and more. The smallest area was for landfill refuse which makes sense as Britain is running out of sites. However, I wonder how much of these items are actually recycled and not just dumped into old quarries etc. When I worked in the local authority sector in the early 1980s, despite having bottle banks, often bottles were just treated like any other household refuse. I assume this practice has changed but how cost effective is it?

The problem of waste disposal was different forty years ago and when I was at primary school even more so.

My mother, like most others, did not have a fridge but a walk-in larder with a marble cold shelf that stayed cool enough year round and rarely did any food go rotten. She used a shopping bag so there were no plastic bags to get rid of.

Our milk and bread were delivered daily. Milk was in reusable glass bottles, delivered by the Co-op man and his horse until the early 1960s.

My father prized the manure left on the road for his roses and vegetable patch!

We did have the luxury of the groceries being delivered by a van with orders being taken by a man each week. I can still remember today that he would have a check list of items and would ask madam 'How are you off for...' say cornflakes, tinned goods and items like flour, soap powder etc. Still much less than those available in supermarkets nowadays. We of course never had any fruit or vegetables that were out of season as they were just not available.

Also kitchen waste, such as potato peelings or old cabbage, ended up on my father's compost heap. So in their way, although they did not know it, most people were very environmentally friendly back in the 1950s. We have gone backwards since then!

In mid-November, Pam had an assessment meeting with her tutor and he confirmed that he was very pleased with her work and her progress. Unlike some of her friends who were in tears after their assessments, she came out smiling which no doubt enhanced her confidence after the problems of the previous summer. In fact she was also pleased that she had been selected to arrange and stage the 2007 exhibition of students' design work that was previously held at a studio in London, at a cost of thirty thousand pounds which was mainly met by sponsors.

After considering several locations, she was proposing to hire the Custard Factory in Birmingham for the following July and a party of five fellow students visited the site to assess their requirements.

The only problem was that her driver on the return trip saw the sign on the motorway for 'M6 north' and ended up in Stoke-on-Trent – hence a fifty mile detour back to Loughborough. Had he taken the M6 south and then the M42 north, several hours would have been saved.

I do appreciate that Birmingham's traffic for visitors and even locals can be confusing. Like most cities in the UK, they have changed so much and continue to with new streets and high-rise buildings. Places I used to visit when I was growing up no longer exist. They call it progress!

Social etiquette since the 1960s has also changed. If you met fellow university friends you would normally shake hands and any expression of intimacy was not really acceptable in public. Smoking in the street was also frowned upon as was kissing, although it was normal for girlfriends/boyfriends to hold hands and the back row of the cinema offered more opportunities then. I wonder if it still does today?

When Pam was at secondary school, I noticed that whenever she met friends in town or on the street etc., there would be a group hug. Today's youth are far less inhibited with showing their affection and whilst we used to do these things in private, it's all so open today.

One thing we did not have was security cameras which are so common today wherever you go. Even most young kids now have camera phones that enable photographs to be sent to their friends within minutes via the internet. Despite all these security measures, it is less safe today in most city and town centres than it was forty years ago. The main difference is that the crime is filmed on CCTV.

Finally, in late November, we visited her house in Loughborough to collect her for a weekend back home.

I have not mentioned previously that her house had a name – 'Rose Villa'. It was an 1850s terraced house which from the front looked small but was really a 'tardis' with six bedrooms, including two en-suite shower rooms.

On entering the old tiled floor of the hall, it was obvious that the occupants were girls as the stairs had shoes of every colour and design on each step – no doubt for a quick getaway!

The lounge area was bright and carefully placed candles adorned the table – obviously a feminine touch. I asked Pam whether she was alone in the house and she said 'probably', so I went in search of the bathroom which in most converted mid-terrace houses is on the ground floor beyond the kitchen. The door was slightly open so in I walked, only to find one of her housemates still in bed although it was nearly twelve noon on a Friday. I think she was quite shocked to see a stranger appear at her door so I apologised and made a swift exit. I realised she was the same girl that I had met last year in the kitchen at Cell Block H when we took Pam for Freshers' Week.

Pam's room on the second floor was just as I imagined, with a steep staircase and sloping walls. However it was a big room, the largest in the house and just like her room back home, in a similar mess.

Unlike her brother Simon, who is very tidy, Pam just does not see the need to maintain order as I am sure can be applied to most of her housemates. Pamela's Law is if you have space on the floor, cover it!

However the overall impression was that it was a good student pad and much better than being in halls; plus she was happy.

With six young women living together for the first time there had to be some arguments but nothing serious – something that you cannot learn without experiencing it and certainly good for their futures.

On her return after the weekend, she was greeted by her friends. "Hi Pam – had a good time? Are we still having munchies at Bernie's tonight?" (This I assume is a local eatery.)

"Of course," said Pamela. Several of the house mates' boy friends were there on that Sunday afternoon but I am not allowed to divulge details for fear of castigation or even worse! I am sure that if I delved deeper there is sufficient material for several books on what goes on at that house.

As chemistry undergraduates in the 1960s, we were regarded as lacking in knowledge of English literature and the arts, so every Friday afternoon we attended tutorials with a lady called Miss Valerie Pitt, a woman of similar stature and mannerisms to the late actress Hattie Jacques.

She was very 'friendly' with the Reverend David Shepherd, the then bishop of Woolwich and later to become bishop of Liverpool. She claimed to have put the fear of God into him, which I could easily believe!

One thing that I did gain from her was a love of the meaning of words and changes in these meanings over time which she referred to as 'semantic shift'. I have mentioned before words such as gay, wicked, cool, mad, rage and many more which today have very different meanings. I am not aware of students today having the same interest in this subject, probably because they themselves participated in developing their own language. The process of change cannot be ignored but I wonder what they are missing.

With Christmas rapidly approaching, I decided that this year we would have a real tree instead of the artificial ones we have had over recent years. As Pam worked during the holidays at our local nurseries I decided to pay them a visit and selected a potted Nordman Fir priced at just twenty-eight pounds (probably two pounds back in 1960?).

I got chatting to one of their staff, a man called Russ, who was about my age and I mentioned my daughter worked in the café during the holidays.

When I mentioned her name, he said, "Oh yes, little Pam, she often speaks to me." When I mentioned that she was at Loughborough University he said his daughter had also been there and stayed in a house-share in the next road to Pam's current property.

What a small world, but more was to come as I found out later that he had been to the same school as my wife, Judith. Amazing! Naturally I asked for a discount at the till and as one of the proprietors he gave me fifty per cent – great, I thought, as my past career had been in procurement. Who says that I cannot still get a good deal?

Feeling very pleased with myself, I carried the Christmas tree to the car but all of a sudden felt a sharp pain in my lower abdomen. A day later, the pain continued and a small lump was present in my groin so I visited the doctor who referred me the next day to a private consultant who confirmed I had an inguinal hernia which needed an operation as it would not get better.

I was booked in with amazing speed for surgery the next Wednesday at our local BUPA hospital. As I no longer had medical insurance, it was to cost me over two thousand pounds – bloody hell, I thought!

I had never had intrusive surgery before and to say the least I was petrified! When the day arrived, I was ushered into a private room and awaited my fate. I can only report that the surgeon, his team and the hospital were excellent but this did not detract from the fact that from the day at the nursery when I felt so good, I would now be having a serious operation.

I had keyhole surgery, with just two small incisions, plus another one in my belly button to pass a fibre optic camera through – a procedure that certainly did not exist back in the 1960s. As well as a general anaesthetic I was also given morphine injections.

My operation took about an hour and I was back home later that night. Conventional hernia surgery in the past would probably entail at least five days in hospital.

My recovery was painful and for the first few days, I took the maximum dose of analgesics which left me feeling weak. All the planned events with friends prior to Christmas had to be cancelled, and again my son Simon had to step into the breach and collect his sister from university for the Christmas break.

The Christmas tree sat proudly in our hall, a reminder of the most expensive item of festive decoration I have ever bought. Two thousand pounds well spent? By Christmas Day I felt much better and my family were acting as my 'servants' so I just sat back and made the most of the occasion! Well why not?

It didn't really feel like a normal Christmas and it was now almost three weeks since I last went out. Pamela was working back at the café and also on her design projects in between. She now really needed an Apple Mac laptop computer and the Bank of Mum and Dad had to foot the thousand-pound bill. The new laptop was amazing, with over a hundred gigabytes of hard-disk drive and a built-in web camera – plus she would be loading design suite software on the system as used by professional graphic designers. Interestingly, this bespoke software was normally priced at eight hundred pounds but students could purchase it with an amazing eighty per cent discount! (Only two hundred pounds – a snip!)

Oh, it had really been an expensive Christmas and I looked forward to a better New Year, certainly health-wise. New Year's Eve, for the first time I can ever remember, was a non-event for me and guess what the first email I opened in the new year was? A company offering cut price Viagra tablets! That was the last thing that I needed at this critical time in my life. How on earth did they obtain my address?

Also at this time, both Pamela and my wife were complaining that the hot water supply in our house was just too hot so I said I would call British Gas to sort it out.

Chapter 6 – Year 2, Term 2

At the end of the second week of January, Pam was back at Loughborough with her housemates. What would this term hold, I asked? Thoughts therefore turned to her forthcoming trip to New York.

Back at our house, the hot water was still boiling so I phoned British Gas under our insurance cover and a service engineer called the same day and confirmed that the motorised valve had a problem and he would replace it shortly.

A week went past and finally he arrived to replace the defective item, a job which was completed within an hour. However, on just looking at the new cable in the airing cupboard and moving it slightly, there was a bright blue spark and the main fuse blew. "Bloody hell!" I said again – that could have killed me!

Having just recovered from my hernia operation, had I been a few millimetres nearer the cable then this could have been the end of me – a sobering thought!

With no apology from British Gas, the same engineer called to rectify the problem! Someone up there must be looking after me!

With Pam having been back at Loughborough for several weeks since Christmas, she was working to complete her projects and we heard very little from her during this time. I think that she was also becoming reluctant to tell me much about her life for fear that it would end up in this book.

I suppose, in hindsight, there was a lot that I did not tell my parents when I was a student in London but of course we did not have the communications that are available today.

Entertainment in the 1960s for poor students like me was in short supply and I remember once that I joined my landlady, Mrs Ivy Dow, and her husband Sid one Wednesday night at the Odeon Bingo in Well Hall, Eltham. No doubt long since gone – or has it?

Having never experienced such an event before, I was amazed at the crowds and the number of bingo cards each player handled. I think that at just twenty years old, the next youngest participant was at least thirty years my senior. Since that evening, I have never attended another such event again.

So it came as a great surprise to find out that my daughter and one of her housemates were, would you believe, also spending a Friday evening at the local bingo hall in Loughborough. History repeating itself again!

As Pam and her friend went in to the hall, everybody looked at them as if they were from another planet. The girls' view of the session was, "The place was full of ageing and weird-looking people hooked on gambling." They even sang 'Happy Birthday' to one lady who was a hundred years old on the day! I doubted if they would visit there again.

It's quite sad in a way that some people gain pleasure from this pastime, but who am I to criticise? As long as they are enjoying themselves!

By early February, Pam had completed her design project which was started back in December and it was time to hand the work in for assessment.

The day arrived and she was called to a one-to-one meeting with her tutor, named Simon. The result was a 2:1 which he explained was quite a step up compared with a failure back in the summer.

I asked if she was going to celebrate her success – perhaps a night at the bingo as she had been given a free ten pound voucher? No, she and her friends would be off to the Union bar in true student fashion! This happened to be half way through her degree course.

The Midlands had its heaviest snow fall for many years, with over ten inches in parts of Birmingham, which brought traffic to a standstill. Loughborough amazingly also had snow but none settled. However, New York had temperatures of minus twelve degrees Celsius and, would you believe, eight foot of snow! Pam had just over a week before her trip so we suggested she purchased a heavy coat which the Bank of Mum and Dad would fund.

She also needed to collect her Apple Mac design suite software so we arranged to meet up in Birmingham which of course included lunch at La Vita, an Italian restaurant which was originally under the name of La Galleria – the first to open up in the city back in 1963.

When I was her age, I can remember huge snow falls in Sutton Coldfield during the 1960s which lasted for weeks. Once, when I was working as a research chemist in Oldbury as part of my work experience, a normal car journey of forty minutes took ten hours and I remember getting home at eleven thirty p.m.

Nothing has changed in this country as to how we deal with ice and snow, unlike other parts of the world.

How would Pam get on in New York City? It would be her second trip, as a few years ago the family had spent New Year's Eve in the Big Apple with several feet of snow.

Pam's flight was on time and I checked the Virgin Atlantic website which confirmed that it arrived at JFK Airport at five p.m. New York time (ten p.m. GMT).

As her mobile would not possibly work in America, we did not hear from her for five days but I had asked her to phone us from Heathrow on her return journey. I checked CEEFAX and her flight landed in London at 8.11 a.m. I felt it would be an hour before she called but as time passed we heard nothing. Perhaps her mobile was broken, or not charged, but around lunchtime the thought occurred as to whether she had boarded the flight.

Being concerned, I decided to contact Virgin at Heathrow, but only had the main telephone number, which was a premium rate automated line which only handled British Airways flight details rather than arrival times for all landings.

Eventually, I found Virgin's London information centre, which to start with was also automated, but after a while I spoke to a human voice who said that passenger lists could not be disclosed, so I asked to speak to her supervisor. After about ten minutes, I again explained the position that all I wanted to know was if my daughter on the New York flight.

The manager, who refused to give her second name, as it was against company policy, stated that under the Data Protection Act details could not be shared. What a waste of time this exercise had been and I wondered if this would have happened when I was Pamela's age. I think not!

Just after two p.m. we did have a very brief call from Pam to say that she was back in Loughborough. Her mobile had not been working and she was suffering with jet lag and felt terrible. We suggested that she tried to sleep it off but I know from past experience that this can be very bad for some people.

Pam's stay in New York had gone well and they managed to pack in a number of visits to the tourist attractions including the Empire State Building and of course essential shopping in Fifth Avenue where several tops, a dress and some shoes were purchased – they were much cheaper than back in England!

Her project was to also photograph signs on buildings, roads and advertising billboards. In all she took a hundred and forty-four photographs and even came back with a length of yellow tape: 'POLICE LINE DO NOT CROSS'. I think that it is better that I did not know how she got hold of this!

Having recovered from her US trip, back at university things were starting to get back to normal. Pam and her friend decided to try the bingo again and she won fifty pounds.

They also missed a gunman on the Saturday night at the Union! Unfortunately, some guy was shot in the stomach and tear gas was also let off at the Union gig. It was probably safer in New York than in downtown Loughborough! I thanked God that she was not involved with the incident, which was mentioned in the Sunday national news.

My wife and I, as you have gathered, enjoyed 1960s pop music and films of that era. For many years, I had been trying to get a copy of the 1968 film 'Here We Go Round the Mulberry Bush' which was based on a book written by Hunter Davies who also wrote the Beatles' memoirs.

The film stared Barry Evans, who has since died and Judy Geeson, Adrienne Posta, Diane Keen, Denholm Elliot, Michael Bates and many other famous actors of the 1960s.

I had tried every avenue, including contacting Hunter Davies, who lives in the Lake District and the USA in the winter. Nobody had a copy of this film.

Hunter Davies I much admire as a writer, and he still has a regular column in the Sunday Times newspaper. I think that we share similar values!

As we also listen to our local radio station, 'Smooth Radio', who mainly play 1960s music, I wrote to one of their DJs, Roger Day. He mentioned my search on air the following Saturday morning. Interestingly, he started his career as a DJ on a pirate radio station off the Essex coast.

With the approach of the end of term, Pam was looking forward to coming home for the Easter holidays and meeting up with her old friends from school and college. I wondered, how long would she keep in touch with them?

When I was her age, I stayed in contact with many of my old pals. But as time went on, with relatives and a family of my own, contact with all but a few of my old friends continued. Some I have known for over fifty years and I often think back to how different the world was back in the fifties and sixties.

Easter, like Christmas, was again a quiet time and Pam had several design projects to complete plus working back at the garden centre. However, she needed to discuss some of the university work with her friend so they decided to stay at the Loughborough house one day in mid-April before the start of the summer term.

Dad therefore offered to drive her there and she could get the train back the next day. The outward journey, as previously, took fifty minutes but on the return, due to road works at Shepshed, I decided to take a different route via the M1 motorway. What a mistake! There had been a serious accident and the motorway had been closed, hence a long diversion which resulted in my arriving back home one hour and thirty minutes late.

The morning on the third week in April, prior to Pam's return for the summer term at Loughborough, was a beautiful day – really warm with not a cloud in the sky.

Pam was back at the café and at home, my wife and I enjoyed a lovely lunch together – what could be more perfect? I have often said that one never quite knows what's round the corner in this life and all was about to happen!

Judith, my wife, said that she would just pop to the loo and then we would go out. Then I heard banging from the cloakroom door. She said, "Jeremy, are you holding the door?" I said no but she was stuck in there with the door firmly shut and I knew that she had always had a fear of being in small spaces. I did not panic and said that I was confident that I would have her out shortly as I collected my tool box from the garage and proceeded to remove the handle.

The problem, I think, was that the mechanism inside the door had broken and despite my efforts, I could not release it. Should I kick in the door in, or could

I? There appeared to be only one solution and that was to phone the emergency services, a task which I had never done before.

On dialling 999, I very quickly got connected and the lady at the call centre said that a fire engine was on its way. A few minutes later, with flashing lights and sirens blazing, they arrived and four big men came down the drive.

The chief fire officer confirmed that they would have to break the door down, but first they would try with a screwdriver – which I had also tried – but this time they were successful and out came Judith after some thirty minutes. How embarrassing: 'a lady locked in the lavatory'!

I was relieved to have her released but my memories went back to when I was at university in the 1960s and when we went on Saturday nights to the local rugby club and sang songs such as that famous one: "Seven old ladies locked in the lavatory – they were there from Monday to Saturday and nobody knew they were there…" of course lubricated with a good glass or more of ale.

Other songs included classics such as 'If I Were the Marrying Kind', 'The Good Ship Venus', 'She was Poor, but She was Honest' and many more. It's strange but I still can remember the words from over fifty years ago!

When Pam came home that afternoon, we had quite a story to tell her and certainly one which my wife would not forget. What if she had been alone in the house, or indeed Pamela or even I had been locked in?

Still, all was sorted out by the brave team in brown.

Chapter 7 – Term 2, Year 3

The house again seemed empty with Pam back at Loughborough for the summer term which was only about six weeks, then over three months' holiday.

With so many twenty-first parties around this time, hardly a week passed without some form of celebration and in the first few days back it was her friend's birthday with the customary meal followed by a club in Loughborough. The dinner was at a local Italian restaurant which did sound a bit dodgy as the meal only cost five pounds.

The place was dirty, with grease-soaked place mats and it was run by a Russian guy. Pam chose Parma ham (or should it have been 'Parma Pam'?) with pasta which she said didn't taste right.

Unfortunately, the following day she had stomach pains and diarrhoea – obviously food poisoning! It was so bad that we decided to collect her and bring her home until she recovered.

A visit to our local GP and various tests confirmed that she did indeed have food poisoning. On her return journey to Loughborough, she also had to see her own doctor on the university campus.

After quite a few problems, we had some good news – Pam had located a copy of the 1960s film, 'Here We Go Round the Mulberry Bush' on an American website – only twenty-nine dollars, so an order was placed. I had been searching the world for this film for at least ten years so I was delighted that she had come up trumps! Perhaps I could inform Roger Day on Smooth Radio?

The summer term was going quickly and Pam had a number of group projects to handle. One was to set up a mock graphic design company with five other students, so she had been tasked with handling the financial aspects. Dad was approached for advice. I don't think she quite appreciated the magnitude of areas to consider. Having started a number of successful new businesses in the past, I was well equipped to answer her questions.

My reply to her was to adopt a tried and tested business planning strategy which I detail below.

Business Planning

Both starting and running a new business are not easy, with many pitfalls! It is important to identify all costs at the beginning and I have produced for you a check list of key factors; plus you might like to consider some of the items detailed in my project management guide which is in the post to you. Please let me have it back one day.

Startup costs:

1. Rental cost of premises

2. Heating and lighting

3. Office cleaning

4. Council tax

5. Public liability insurance (staff, visitors, customers etc)

6. Risk insurance – what if your company give the wrong advice to customers and they incur costs and sue you?

7. Office wages and directors' fees

8. Advertising and marketing costs (including 'event organising')

9. Motor and travelling expenses

10. Website setup costs

11. PCs, phones, mobiles and technology

12. Stationery, office furniture and fittings (e.g. letterheads, compliment slips and business cards)

13. Bank interest charges (loan costs?)

14. Accountancy charges plus VAT registration, costs for producing annual balance sheet, current financial liabilities/assets, accruals and capital account

15. Record keeping including VAT and estimate of net annual profit (profit and loss accounting)

16. Depreciation of vehicles and other assets (net book value)

17. Staff training costs

18. Compliance with health and safety and other government legislation (and there is a lot!)

19. Sundry expenses

It is important that you have a business plan perhaps over five years, together with estimated turnover/growth per year. When will the company expect to break even and move into profit? What is your target market? Your local chamber of commerce can offer a lot of help to a new business – check details on the internet.

Also there are many books, as you can imagine, on the subject of starting a new business.

I have also run a number of sessions for companies on what is known as SWOT Analysis, which in essence identifies strengths, weaknesses, opportunities and threats to the business. No company should contemplate starting a new business without conducting this procedure and it should be the number one task on your business plan. I would be pleased to let you have more details on this if you want.

Good Luck! Love, Dad.

The Dragons' Den would have been proud of me!

Given the time available, I felt that she could only just scratch the surface, but I felt that the university was right to let the students find out about these things as in their future careers almost certainly they would need this information.

Running your own business is not easy, as I know from personal experience and you would be amazed at the number who fail in their first year. The figure has also increased significantly since we have had the COVID-19 virus worldwide.

The other major task which Pam and her colleagues were organising was the summer graphic design show but the original venue of the Custard Factory in Birmingham had to be changed because of the costs. The new site was to be the Works Gallery in Digbeth, Birmingham. They were also designing a website with the name 'The Love Hate Show' with forty-nine of her fellow students taking part. My wife and I would certainly pay a visit to the show which was going to be held over a five-day period in early June.

It was interesting to note that over sixty per cent of them were girls. When I was a student, there was only one girl on our chemistry course: a Miss Ann Holder, who I remember had a very protective mother. The few brave guys who asked her out had first to be vetted by Mom and Ann had to phone her mother every hour to confirm that she was OK and that was long before we had mobile phones! I often wonder what happened to Ann.

In fact it would also be interesting to hear what my university colleagues are doing now. My closest friend was Bob Ball, a rugby player, and the last I heard of him he was in Germany working for a pharmaceutical company. I seem to recall that he was sharing a house with a blonde German girl called Heidi! He always attracted the best-looking females.

In early June we attended Pam's graphic design show at 'The Works' gallery in Digbeth, Birmingham. This was an area which I knew well back in the sixties.

In fact I took one of my first girlfriends, Lynne, on a date to the Silver Blades Ice Rink which also had a nightclub above it called 'The Heartbeat'. Here they had ultraviolet lighting which was popular at the time. Any girls wearing white bras under their tops would show up and become highly visible! I cannot remember if Lynne wore a white bra at the time!

In the charts, back in 1964, was a song by the McCoys, 'Hang on Sloopy' which now whenever I hear it brings back memories of the Silver Blades Ice Rink and club. Unfortunately the place is now boarded up and derelict. The last I heard of Lynne was that following the breakup of her first marriage to a guitarist, she had moved to Canada to live with her brother Mike and family.

Back at 'The Love Hate Show' we were quite impressed with the standard of the students' work and although the building was old they made the best use of the space. Very similar to the Dragons' Den venue! Being one of the organisers, Pam was quite pleased with how the event had turned out. Her own work depicted various illustrations of love such as 'love is in the air', 'love hurts', 'love is a drug', 'love is blind' and 'love is sweet' all on canvas.

The following week, on her return to Loughborough, she would be collecting the results of all her second-year work projects. Last year of course she had to retake one of the modules so it was a nail-biting time!

On the Monday afternoon, she rang us in an excited state – yes, she had been given a first – amazing! Both my wife and I were delighted; this proved that given effort, she could achieve great results. I was sure this would bolster her confidence for the future.

Whilst not going into detail, the six girls in the house, who had got on so well for the last year were now having arguments – particularly around who should clean the property when they left – all part of life's experience!

After several days of partying and celebrations, it was time to head home for the summer vacation and as usual the vast amount of luggage, art materials and electrical equipment had to be transported back. I thought Pam had a lot of clothes but she said some of the other girls' parents had to make several journeys!

Back at home, we quickly became used to having our daughter around although she was out most days either working or meeting with her old friends from school and college.

We also attended my friend Graham's sixty-first birthday party and met up with our friends, many of whom we first met in the 1960s. Back in 1968, I had made an eight millimetre movie film called 'Securing the Prize' directed by me, 'Jerry Fellini', which Graham had converted to DVD. This was shown at the party and it was interesting to see how people had changed over the last forty years!

At the time, four of us – Graham, Dave, Terry and I – used to meet every Monday for a drink at our local pub, and we each contributed twenty pence per week with the first one of us getting married winning the prize. It was called the Monday Night Drinkers' Club (MNDC) and hence the name of my film, 'Securing the Prize'.

One of the most amazing nights we had was when Terry, who used to own an old grey Minivan, turned up in a new car. He asked me to guess what it was and after many tries I gave up. He then took me into the car park and there it was: an opalescent blue E-type Jaguar. I was staggered – and of course it featured in my film.

Even then it was a classic car and still is. By the way, the winner of the MNDC prize was me when I tied the knot with Judith back in April 1975. I seem to remember that the fund was around twenty pounds, which back then was quite a lot of money. All the 'old' members of the MNDC are now married and have children of their own, or rather should I say, grown up sons and daughters.

Time does certainly move on fast!

Pam continued to work long hours at the garden centre café but was pleased to be building up some savings for her final year at Loughborough Uni. As you can imagine, all sorts of people visit the café and there are some characters, such as the elderly lady who comes in every week complaining of a different illness – she has been nicknamed 'Mrs Arthritis'!

There is the couple who visit every Saturday without fail, arriving for breakfast, staying for lunch and then having afternoon tea. Another is 'Psychic Woman' who reads palms and has four cappuccinos, one after the other.

Then there was the case of the disappearing teapots, which were tracked down to a mother and daughter who insisted on having china ware rather than stainless steel. Eventually they were caught red-handed at the door by the manager, who found the stolen item in their bag. They were told never to be seen again on the premises. A waitress certainly sees life!

The summer was late coming that year and both June and July were the wettest on record, with extensive flooding, particularly in Worcestershire as rivers such as the Severn and Avon burst their banks.

There was a new prime minister in place, Gordon Brown. Since he had taken control, things had started to go wrong – a car bomber at Glasgow Airport, rain and flooding, more soldiers killed in Iraq, share prices dropping and now in August Britain had foot and mouth disease back in Surrey. Bring back Tony Blair – I think not!

It was now mid-August and the summer had finally arrived. Pam had been invited to stay with her friend in Milan where he worked for the fashion house Prada as part of his degree at Manchester University in history and Italian studies. He hoped to then complete a law degree and he obviously spoke the language fluently. Pam had first met him when they were in sixth form together some five years ago and they were still friends.

The trip to Milan was paid for again from the Bank of Mum and Dad. When she arrived there, the temperature was around thirty-four degrees and too hot to do much! On the Saturday they went to Lake Garda which she said was beautiful and had views of the snow-topped Alps.

Milan is a similar size to Birmingham and in August, like many European countries, almost everyone leaves the city for the coast and the lakes. This explains why on the return trip there were only nine people on the flight. It was also Pam's first trip on her own and she enjoyed the break from waitressing.

When she arrived back at Birmingham Airport, we were there to meet her. She had had a good time in Milan but all the walking had injured her feet, and the only comfortable shoes were her black high heels – which because of the heat, she wore with a miniskirt and no tights. Unfortunately, at Milan Airport, several nuns were pointing at her as they thought she was a prostitute! Italians can be very strait-laced, particularly the older ones!

As predicted, she came home with a new handbag and designer jeans – she really can't resist shopping, unlike her father!

In September, there were further problems for the government. There was a major crisis at Northern Rock Bank, with long queues of customers trying to take their savings out. Two billion was cashed in just three days. Their shares dropped by over eighty per cent, and the FTSE also plummeted as did most world stock markets.

This never happened when I was her age. With the daylight hours reducing and the end of summer approaching, Pam prepared for her last year at uni.

This last twelve months had been good for Pam, with work and travel taking her to London, Birmingham, New York and Milan – something that I did not do when I was studying.

So what would the next year hold for her?

Chapter 8 – Year 3, Term 1

Pam's final year at Loughborough University was due to start and this time next year she hopefully would have graduated and be starting her career in graphic design, probably in London. Both our 'children' will by then have fled the nest and we will be on our own again. How will life be, I pondered?

This year she moved into a new house with just three of her mates. Their rooms are smaller but generally better decorated and furnished. The journey back passed without incident and the volume of her luggage appeared to be less but she had left some items with her friend. In my final year at uni in London, I had my own car so my father did not have the regular trek back and forth. As with my daughter, it was usually packed full for the journey down to London.

My final year was, on reflection, one of my best years and I thought – where would I be after graduation? Would I stay in London? Would I continue being a chemist?

Thinking about furniture back in the 1960s, unlike today there were few choices in terms of quality products at reasonable prices. Slowly this changed with particular influence from Scandinavian countries like Denmark and Sweden.

Three materials came together: teak wood, glass and stainless steel. Cheaper furniture was available but did not last, although to many young people this did not matter.

A new throwaway society had arrived and with the impact today of environmental concerns we appear to be returning to traditional values. Certainly in the sixties there were no DIY stores such as B&Q, Homebase and others. If you wanted wood, you went to a timber merchant; paint and wallpaper, to a decorators'; and anything else to a high street ironmonger who sold almost everything from screws to locks and tools. I always remember every shop smelt of paraffin and gardening chemicals and the owner always knew exactly the location of thousands of items. Unfortunately, very few of these ironmongers are now left as competition has forced them out of business.

In just two days of being back at Loughborough, Pam had got herself a job paying sixty to seventy pounds per day selling local shops/restaurants discount cards to freshers. Each card was twenty pounds, which entitled the holder to three years of discounts at a range of retail outlets in Loughborough. She was delighted to take on this task.

It was now early October and Royal Mail were on strike – something which was a regular occurrence back in the 1960s and 1970s.

I remember my first job as a commercial management trainee for a Midlands-based chemical company. A lot of our business was conducted in Europe and when the postal strike started in England, I was tasked with travelling with the urgent mail to France.

I drove to Folkestone in Kent, staying the night in Ashford on the way and caught the morning ferry to Boulogne. There I met with our French agent, Mademoiselle Marie-Therese Piquet from the Paris office.

As I walked from the port into the town, I felt like a spy meeting up with the French Resistance during the Second World War. It was quite exciting!

We met outside a cafe and exchanged mail before going for lunch at a seafood restaurant where I tried my first 'soupe de poisson' – fish soup. This experience I will never forget. It started my passion for French food and as a family we have been back to France many times over the years.

I often wonder what happened to Mademoiselle Piquet.

Just a few days into the new term, Pam's friend had been diagnosed with glandular fever and swollen tonsils so her mother came to collect her and take her back home to recover. The illness can take from two weeks to several months to subside and Pam was really missing her company so at the moment there were only four girls in the house.

Pam's main graphic design project this term was to market information to people about Alzheimer's disease, a subject close to her heart as her gran (my wife's eighty-four-year-old mother) was suffering at the time from the advanced stages of the illness.

It was very sad, as she was in a wheelchair, could not do anything for herself and had lost the ability to speak. So I think that the more people are aware of this terrible disease the better.

I would be interested to see Pam's final drawings and posters. Back in the 1960s, this illness was not recognised and most were eventually admitted to mental institutions. It must have been grim! I believe the government and the NHS should do more to help these people.

On November 5th, Pam and her friends attended the Union's firework display. Today there are fewer private displays but in the 1960s they were the norm. I remember many occasions when my friends and I built big bonfires in our back gardens. Our mums cooked loads of baked potatoes, sausages and beans and made fizzy drinks.

I remember the fireworks being laid out on the kitchen table which was really warm and cosy as we had an AGA cooker. It is still exactly the same design today and unchanged for over fifty years – even the thermometer on the front is identical, as are the hob covers. Today an Aga sells for over five thousand pounds!

They were magic times! For five pounds you could buy a big box of fireworks including rockets. Today, some of the individual fireworks can cost thirty pounds or more each! So the cost of putting on a display must be huge.

One thing we had in the 1960s, which I don't think are available today, are thunder-crackers or bangers. They were really powerful and made a lot of noise. Placed inside a tin they could easily burst the sides open – quite dangerous when I think back – which is probably why they have ceased manufacture. No doubt health and safety!

Pam had not been back home for over eight weeks now and we were missing her but Christmas was not far away. However, out of the blue came a phone call in early November saying could she come home for a short stay, so of course we said yes, and this also gave me more information for this book.

Her project on Alzheimer's disease awareness was progressing and soon Pam and her colleague were planning to launch seventy helium balloons at dusk, each one containing a bright diode light and a paper message detailing the website they had set up. It would look spectacular and they planned to film the event.

The finished project would be exhibited at a London gallery the following year in the city where over six thousand students would mount a show of their work.

Over the last few months, the media had covered the Madeleine McCann disappearance case every day and what I did not realise is that the independent forensics expert was a Dr Ron Denney, based in Kent: the very same man who was my analytical chemistry lecturer in London back in the 1960s. What a small world it is and also one of this gentleman's claims to fame was that he invented the 'breathalyser', now used by police forces throughout the world.

I don't think that he made a lot of money from this at the time. I also remember him trying to persuade me to stay in chemistry rather than move to a career in business; I often wonder how my life would have been different had I not changed my career path.

Back at Loughborough, Pam and her colleagues were putting the final preparations together for the balloon launch that was to take place on the first Monday of December.

When the day arrived, the weather conditions appeared to be perfect, with clear skies and a light breeze. Throughout the day, all the balloons were prepared and filled with helium gas from a cylinder they had hired.

Pam also contacted East Midlands Air Traffic Control to advise them of 'lights in the sky'. I wonder if any aircraft spotted them?

A party of people had been invited to the launch site by one of Loughborough's sports pitches. Several photographers were there to film the event. All seventy balloons were enclosed in a large net that was held down by just five stakes.

However, disaster struck as a sudden gust of wind blew almost half of the balloons into the sky. Panic ensued as they had not started to film. So the final launch a short while later was only about thirty balloons and although it was recorded, it was far from the spectacular event they had planned. Pam was very disappointed in view of the effort and cost of the project.

As I said to Pam, at least all the balloons went up in the sky! I await the results on their website.

I could tell that Pam was stressed and like many students in their final year, the lecturers put more pressure on them which was exactly the same when I was at university.

At the time you think it's wrong, but with the benefit of hindsight you see that it does prepare you for the real world which I am sure today is a much tougher one. I can imagine that graphic designers have tight deadlines to meet and next Easter Pam was about to find out as she was to gain work experience at a professional studio in the city of Liverpool. Should be interesting!

It was only about a week before she came home for Christmas and we were looking forward to hearing about her studies and experiences of the last term.

Christmas had arrived and Pam was back home but having to work hard on her Alzheimer's project plus her job as a waitress at the garden centre.

This last term had been expensive and as funds were low, she needed all the money she could get. She also had some urgent research work and needed to visit our local library.

She said, can you believe that they were playing Christmas carols on a CD player and the librarians were singing along as they stamped the books on loan – or rather scanned the barcodes, as the former procedure went out back in the early 1970s. So much for being quiet in the library.

Long gone are the days when you were told to be quiet in the library! The biggest change has been the introduction of computers, where members are allowed to browse the internet and send/receive emails free of charge. I wonder if, in time, books will become superfluous. The world is already a very different place since I was a student in the 1960s – not all for the better I believe.

Today was New Year's Eve and Pam had gone back to Loughborough for a student party and would be back home for just a few days before her return for her penultimate term.

Again, this Christmas had been quiet for us and I suppose as one gets older it loses its magic, although like most families, we still have a turkey lunch with all the trimmings and of course exchange presents. Pam wanted money so her main present was a cheque. On looking back at previous Christmases, the key factor was children, and so as they grow up, something is missing. What we need now is grandchildren and although I drop many hints, the message falls on deaf ears!

I wondered what 2008 would hold for us all?

Chapter 9 – Year 3, Term 2

After a non-eventful Christmas, Pam was now back at Loughborough and had moved into a larger bedroom at the house for the remainder of her time at university. It had a large desk, so no doubt she would quickly fill the space as usual. Work had become more intense and she was busy producing a seven-thousand-word dissertation which had to be presented in February with the marks awarded counting towards her final degree. The subject was to assess the importance of the use of shock images in advertising, as used for example by 'United Colors of Benetton' and particularly charity organisations. At the same time, she was working with her colleague on the Alzheimer's project.

Back at home, we had almost become used to her not being there, although the day she went back to Loughborough remained a sad one for my wife and me. The dark mornings and damp weather conditions also did not help but I am sure that we were not alone.

As mentioned previously, in the 1960s I worked as a chemist on nuclear magnetic resonance spectroscopy which led on to developing magnetic resonance imaging

(MRI). MRI is used today at hospitals as a diagnostic tool, which unlike x-ray, uses no ionising radiation.

Following my hernia operation just before Christmas the year before, I had been experiencing some pain in my left side which my consultant felt was not another hernia but could be related to my hip, so it was proposed that I had a MRI scan at our local hospital, but this time on the NHS. Little did I even think forty years ago, when I worked on this technology, that I would be in the centre of a huge magnet receiving a scan.

When the day arrived, although I knew about what might happen, I was still a little nervous. It was interesting to talk with the radiologist about how I was involved with this technology in the past. The machine is a huge magnet about the size of a van with a hole in the middle where one lies whilst the equipment scans a particular body section.

Each machine costs over £1.5 million with substantial running and maintenance costs. For those technically minded, it had a magnetic field strength of 1.5 tesla and moveable radio frequency coils which could be positioned to scan different parts of the body.

To those who have not experienced this technology, it is not a discomfort but I can understand that some patients might find it claustrophobic. Although I did not know at the time, my wife, who was waiting for me, overheard a conversation with the receptionist who was talking to a nervous patient on the phone and she said, "It's nothing to worry about and you can come and see it beforehand – but I must admit I would not want to be in the machine!" How unprofessional!

Two things did come as a surprise to me: firstly that it takes about thirty minutes and it is also very noisy. The tapping sound is like a machine gun going off as if you are in a war zone. But they do provide patients with headphones and you can bring along your favourite CD.

I thought long and hard as to which I should choose. Maybe Meat Loaf's 'Bat out of Hell' or the French synthesiser performer Jean Michael Jarre's 'Oxygene'. This latter piece of music was played for astronauts on the space shuttle.

Pam thought that neither of these were appropriate and that I should have some relaxing music so I chose some classical baroque music which I like. In hindsight, Jean Michael Jarre would have been perfect in a space-age sort of way! Maybe if I have another scan.

The time passed quite quickly but I was a little relieved when the radiologist said the procedure was finished as it can be surprisingly hard to lie perfectly still strapped to a moving bed for half an hour. I now awaited the results from my consultant.

Pam's dissertation of eight thousand, four hundred and twenty-five words on the use of 'shock tactics' in advertising was now complete and handed in on Friday in mid-February. She now had a new project: 'Selling the Sunday Times newspaper to young people', to which I should love to make a serious contribution, having read this excellent publication since around the mid-1960s.

On the downside, Pam's friend had been in an accident with her car, but apart from minor injuries she was OK. As I have said, you never know what's round the bend in this world.

I should now like to move on to the subject of sex! I can honestly say that I had very little detail about Pam's relationships since she had been at university – but not without trying, I might add! However, back when I was a student in London the world was a very different place. The contraceptive pill had just become available and some student girls took advantage of this facility, but only a few used this method, so I was led to believe.

We had the beginnings of a sexual revolution which was about to change the world. This was at the same time as miniskirts, flower power and soft drugs that were appearing in 'swinging London' and California. In many ways, this was a magic time but as chemistry students we had serious work to complete in our final year at uni (except the latter was always referred to as college or university).

During that time, my relationships with girls were generally short term and I was, like many of my close student friends, focused on gaining my degree – unlike some other of my colleagues.

I always remember one guy, at the Saturday night discos, who each week would dance with a girl and ask the same question: "Do you drop 'em?" He usually got his face smacked, but not always! I often wonder what happened to him! Maybe he's now in the government!

It was now the second week of an unseasonably warm February and Pam phoned, all excited. Her Alzheimer's project was marked as first class by the university and she was delighted. All she needed now was a good mark on her dissertation and she would probably graduate with at least an upper second. Naturally we were very pleased.

Two weeks after the MRI scan, my consultant phoned me with the good news that all was normal, which was a huge weight off my mind.

On the Wednesday of the last week of February, England had been hit by an earthquake at 5.3 magnitude on the Richter scale – the biggest in the UK for twenty-five years! Although I am a light sleeper, I did not notice this in Sutton Coldfield.

Pam phoned the following morning to say that it woke everyone in the road, with her bed shaking and items falling off the shelves in her room. As you can imagine, the girls were all very frightened and several people went out onto the streets at around one a.m.

The quake was centred on Market Rasen, some fifty-nine miles from Loughborough. It was felt as far north as Aberdeen, as far west as Cardiff and as far south as the Isle of Wight.

Nobody was quite sure at the time what caused it, although the movement of tectonic plates was the most likely cause. I never remember such events in the 1960s although I understand that Britain has over two hundred minor tremors each year.

Pamela was home on a weekend for her twenty-second birthday and we all went out for dinner on the Saturday night to a local restaurant – the food was excellent!

I couldn't believe that next term would be her last at university. How quickly these three years had gone.

She was a very different person now and much more confident. I believe the experience had been beneficial, particularly living away from home and looking after herself, something which I too went through when I was her age.

When we graduated in the late 1960s, very few people had degrees, but for the young of today it is a very different position. I believe that having experienced living away from home, Pamela will never quite be the same again but she will always be our daughter and we will continue to offer her our love and support.

I remember that, following my graduation, I had very little difficulty getting a job and had many offers including from a dyestuffs producer in London and a major pharmaceutical company called Pfizer, with plants and offices throughout the world. This same company are today producing the coronavirus vaccine.

I decided to move from being an analytical chemist to a position as a commercial management trainee with a Midlands-based chemical company, which also included a company car – a white Ford Escort.

I think at the time I was one of the first of my friends to have a company car. The position was initially involved with chemical sales but at some time in the future I would become a purchasing manager for feedstock oils and chemicals. This of course led to my career in buying, something which I have never regretted. I wonder where my daughter Pamela will finish up?

With the end of term approaching, Pam's main task was to complete her projects, including designing her own website. She would only be home for the Easter break for just one day before her trip to Liverpool for a week's work experience at a design studio called 'Smiling Wolf'.

She would be staying in a local hotel which she was in the process of booking, together with train tickets, over the internet. I believe the experience will be useful although naturally she was a bit apprehensive before the trip.

The 'local hotel' Pam had chosen was the world-famous Adelphi which she felt had seen better days but was clean and cheap. The first Adelphi Hotel dates back to 1827 and today's building is the third incarnation and was opened in 1914 on the eve of the outbreak of World War One. It was to be the last city hotel that the railways ever built and it still has many special architectural features. Many famous people have stayed there including kings, queens, presidents, and film and pop stars. Sir Winston Churchill and indeed Harold Wilson were also regular visitors. Rumour has it that Adolf Hitler worked as a waiter there for a short time when he was a twenty-year old visiting his cousin. Whether or not that is true I am not sure but it makes for a good story.

There is now a major renovation programme taking place to return the Adelphi to its former glory. Pam's room was massive, as was the marbled bathroom, but she felt the whole building looked tired. It's certainly a big hotel, with over four hundred en-suite bedrooms, a leisure club with an indoor swimming pool and several restaurants. The conference capacity is around eight hundred delegates and the banqueting facility can cater for seven hundred people. The hotel was also only five minutes' walk from where she would be working.

Her main tasks were to shadow some of the graphic designers, attend meetings and of course make tea and coffee. This is something of which she had a lot of previous experience in as a waitress at the garden centre! The week passed quickly and gave her some valuable experience to include on her CV.

Pam was then back home for Easter and apart from completing other project work, she resumed her role as a waitress. This work was likely to be her last before finishing her degree and her plan was not to return to waitressing. However, the money this brought in was very welcomed as this last term had been very expensive and she was well into her bank overdraft, as were most of her fellow students. I was very lucky that during the whole of my time in London during the 1960s, I never had a student loan or overdraft, which of course is the norm today.

The lesson of managing money was something that has never left me and I always attempt to live within my means, even now, fifty years on.

I could never live now as I did when I was a student, as one becomes accustomed to a certain standard of living and reducing it is very hard.

Pam has adapted well to living as a 'poor' student, something that we hope she will also appreciate in the future.

Over Easter, Pam attended a colleague from work's wedding service at a local church. She also had some good news from a job application, the details of which she found lying around the studio at Loughborough. What caught her eye was that the location was in her home town of Sutton Coldfield and coincidentally I also knew the person who was the owner of the promotion and events agency. However, I did not know him well and we had only met briefly years ago.

Pamela, having sent off her CV and other details, was delighted to be on the second selection list which required her to complete a small project and present her findings and views at an interview which was to be held at Millennium Point in Birmingham.

The building had been built in the year 2000 and included many technological innovations and exhibits, including a state of the art 'IMAX' cinema.

For anyone who has not seen films in this format, you would be stunned by the amazing clarity and screen size which literally appears to fill the room as if you are actually experiencing events live.

Pam thought that the interview was good but sadly she did not secure the post and was naturally disappointed. Whatever the reason, I did feel that the experience of her first 'real' interview would be beneficial in the future – apparently none of her friends on her course had a job offer yet. It was going to be a tough time ahead, particularly with Britain heading towards a recession.

The final term was going slowly; Pam had a number of projects to complete but as mentioned previously, one never knows what's round the corner in life. This time it was not good news as one of her housemates had stress problems. I am, as I said to Pam, sure that this was not her fault or indeed problem but she still felt bad at the time.

This is very sad for someone so young. We all hoped that she would recover but I thought she had possibly lost her chance of gaining a degree at Loughborough – which is even more tragic that this has happened in her last term. I often think that dealing with any problems is hard at this critical time.

If someone has a broken arm or leg, one can sympathise but with mental stress it is very different because you cannot see any injury.

My graduation ceremony was a very low-key affair which started at around six thirty p.m. and finished by eight p.m., followed by a buffet and drinks (particularly sherry) with the vice-chancellor and heads of departments and faculties.

I cannot remember the reason my parents did not attend as indeed those of most of my friends did not either. I do remember after the event, all my group of friends, around fifteen new graduates, went round to the pub for a final drink together. It was in many ways a sad occasion as most of us would never meet up again, although of course we said we would keep in touch.

Chapter 10 – The Graduation

On a hot, sultry, July day we set out with Pamela for what was likely to be our last trip to Loughborough. It appeared almost like yesterday when we first took her for Freshers' Week three years before in September. How quickly time goes. The graduation ceremony was to be held in a huge sports hall on the university campus, the latter of which stretched for miles over most of the town. As we drove through the many car parks, I was impressed with the attention to detail and the current students were on hand to direct us to the hall.

Firstly, Pam had to obtain her gown and although we had arrived with plenty of time to spare, the queues of graduands and families were growing and blocking the walkways around the buildings. Pam eventually arrived, smiling, in her flowing gown and I was particularly struck by the number of girls, who appeared to outnumber the boys by ten to one. I learnt later that of the four hundred who graduated from the School of Art and Design, less than five per cent were male.

When I graduated in 1970, less than one per cent were female – few girls went to university in the 1960s.

Now, in 2008, as we entered the massive sports hall which had been decorated with large banners of Loughborough University, we separated from Pamela and sat with the other parents, some of which had also brought with them grandparents.

Without exception, everyone had a video or still digital camera. I felt at the time it was good that I did not bring my old 35 mm SLR camera, so we borrowed Pamela's almost state-of-the art compact digital one. She would then print off copies of photos for us. Would they be viewed again?

As we waited for the procession to enter the hall, 'Music for the Royal Fireworks' by G.F. Handel was played on what I think was an electronic organ by the appropriately named Mr John Keys, MA, LRAM, ARCM, ARCO – to give him his official status.

Then, as the entourage of university hierarchy and their guests, plus around four hundred graduands, entered the hall, the music of Charles-Marie Widor's 'Marche Pontificale' boomed out across the room. Following the chancellor, Sir John Jennings', welcoming address, the process of conferring degrees began and went on for over an hour and ten minutes.

I had been warned previously about how boring this can be and although I started clapping for each new graduate, after a while my hands began to ache. Unlike the gentleman behind me who clapped very loudly, continuously, about a couple of feet from my ears.

Among the other awards was one for chef Mr Terry Brookes in recognition of his service and commitment to the university catering for over forty years. No doubt much deserved, for feeding what must have been millions of hungry students and staff over the past four decades.

After some two hours, the audience rose as the procession began to leave the hall again with accompanying organ music – this time a Theodore Dubois toccata.

As we left the hall and met up again with Pamela, I was very thirsty but the only items on sale at a small, tented bar were plastic mugs of coffee and tea plus packets of biscuits. The area where hundreds graduates and their proud parents poured out of the hall was a building site covered with stones and rubble.

It looked a sorry state, particularly as the chancellor in his robes and his equally brightly adorned guests tried to mingle with the crowd. I can imagine better surroundings at a minor Russian university in the Urals, if they have one.

I have only been to a few graduation ceremonies but they were fun events with jazz bands playing, sun umbrellas, balloons and people supping summer drinks in a carnival type atmosphere.

At Loughborough, nothing!

The brochure which accompanied the invitations, entitled 'Let's celebrate', detailed some catering arrangements including a barbecue on the lawn of the walled garden on the other side of the Loughborough campus. Unfortunately I had left the map in the car. Despite asking, nobody, including my daughter, knew where it was and although there were student marshals around on arrival, they now seemed to have disappeared. What an appalling lack of organisation. Surely someone could have been around to direct the proceedings.

Then we learnt that as there were both morning and afternoon ceremonies, we would have to wait for at least an hour or more for the barbecue, as 'sitting B' – assuming we could get a place.

At this point, my thirst got the better of me and after Pam had said her goodbyes to her friends we left the university, almost certainly for the last time and headed towards a country pub which she recommended. As the three of us went into the restaurant area of the 'Quorndon Fox', we were met by friendly staff who directed us to a table.

As I sipped my glass of cold Chardonnay, my thoughts turned back to that day three years ago when we first took Pamela to Loughborough. However, this time it was different as we were the only 'table for three' in the restaurant.

As the chancellor of Loughborough University said to all those students who had been with them for three years or more, "This is both the end of an era and the beginning of their new lives and careers – I wish them well for the future."

I often wonder what the future now holds.